A Wilding Year

IN MEMORY OF
Edward Dale
AND
Dianne Fuller

BRINGING LIFE BACK TO THE LAND

A Wilding Year

BATSFORD

HANNAH DALE

Introduction

In 2015, my husband Jack inherited a small farm in Lincolnshire. It was unexpected and unwanted – the result of his dad's short and intense battle with a brain tumour that took a kind and inspirational man far too soon.

The land Jack inherited possesses in abundance what his dad affectionately referred to as 'character'. Claimed from marshy wetlands by the drainage experts of the 17th century, it is stubborn ground that does not want to be cajoled into producing food for its human custodians. It is clear that the land wants to embrace its natural inclination to be wet, despite the best efforts of land drains and ditches. Much of it sits under water during the winter before the clay soil bakes hard in the summer, opening up deep fissures and strangling anything that tries to grow in its inhospitable tilth.

Despite the challenges, for the first few years we tried unsuccessfully to generate a profitable harvest from the land. The stress of watching the weather is an occupational hazard for all farmers, and it is invariably too wet, too hot, too cold or too dry at any one time, but the frustration of watching a crop of winter wheat drown under stagnant water, or trying to persuade a seed to germinate on dusty baked-hard ground, was painful and we started to think about other ways the land might be used.

In 2018, Jack read *Wilding* by Isabella Tree, a book that documents the transformation of an unprofitable arable farm over a period of 20 years into a rich mosaic of habitats offering refuge to a large number of species clinging on to the last vestiges of suitable territory that exist at the fringes of the environment we have shaped. The principle of 'rewilding' is to restore ecosystems to the point that nature can take care of itself and we both found the book and the concept incredibly inspiring. We felt that our poor, unproductive land was an ideal candidate for rewilding. Rather than losing money year after year trying to grow crops, it could be better put to use for the benefit of nature. We also felt that it was a fitting way to honour Jack's dad, who loved the countryside and was an early pioneer of regenerative farming. He had spent a large part of his career developing a seed drill that negates the need for ploughing, thereby protecting the soil structure and preserving his beloved earthworms in the process.

As a wildlife illustrator and having studied Zoology at Cambridge University, I spend much of my time in the Lincolnshire countryside, and the idea of allowing our farm to stop fighting against its natural instincts and letting nature flow back in was incredibly appealing. Over the past few years, I can't be alone in having experienced severe anxiety related to the climate and biodiversity emergencies that we are facing, and the catastrophic collapse of so many species that shows no sign of abating. The loss of wildlife abundance we have experienced in Britain has outpaced almost everywhere else in the world*, and a re-setting of expectations establishes a new baseline for each generation, meaning that we can't even remember what we have lost. Far from being a stable situation, many species are still in free fall and without the protection that exists from being part of a large colony or connected, functioning ecosystem, the few isolated breeding pairs still clinging on to fragments of habitat that remain have little hope of recovery. Successful reintroductions and an overwhelming love of the natural world among the British people offer beacons

---

*According to analysis of more than 58,000 species undertaken by the Natural History Museum that showed the UK has only half of its entire biodiversity left, putting it in the bottom 10 per cent of the world's countries.

of hope, but the slow response of government and denials from people who prefer to bury their heads in the sand or have vested interests in maintaining the status quo, are both frustrating and heart-wrenching.

In July 2019, we took the final harvest from our soil and tentatively stood back to see what would happen. We planted trees, dug ponds and scattered locally sourced, native wildflower seeds to try and replenish the depleted seedbank. Above all, we began allowing the land to express its own character, and to start the process of healing itself.

Ceasing cultivation, spraying and fertilizing is now allowing the regeneration of scrub, a vital habitat largely missing from our countryside. Within a few short years, our unfettered hedgerows are now festooned with blossom in spring and burgeoning with berries in autumn. The soils crawl and the grasses fizz with insects. In summer, clouds of meadow brown butterflies numbering well over a thousand billow over patches of creeping thistles. The birdsong in spring has exploded in volume as more food availability means more successful breeding seasons. Barn owls hunt over messy grass wriggling with voles where once a sterile bed nursed its monoculture of wheat, like a meadow pipit feeding a cuckoo chick in its nest that doesn't belong there.

As an artist, our return to wildness has provided me with an unlimited source of inspiration, and spending time on the farm with a sketchbook provides both a cathartic relief from the stresses of daily life and a source of new paintings. My artwork has always been inspired by nature, interwoven with a dose of imagination for good measure and this book is both a journal and a sketchbook, capturing glimpses of the characters that have joined us here at Low Farm over the course of a year. I hope that bringing them to life in both words and art encourages more people to see beauty in an untidy landscape and to embrace a little more wildness in their lives.

Vicar's Field

Ings Field

Barn

The Track

Ponds

The Park

Basin Wood

Fox Cover

The Beck

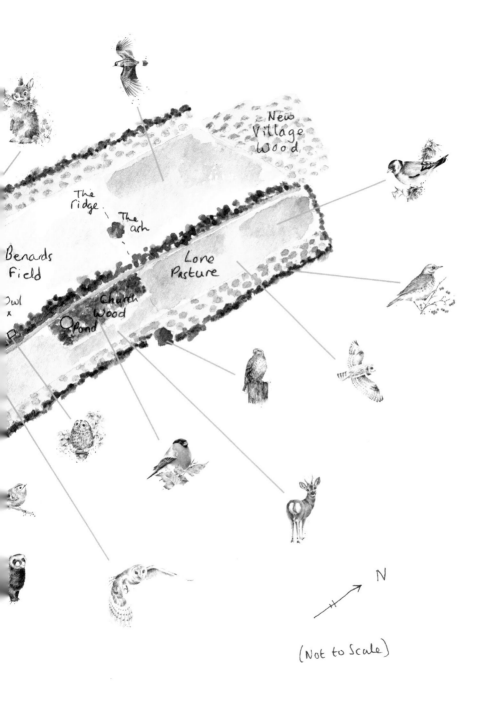

New Village Wood

The ridge

The ash

Benards Field

Owl ✗

Church Wood

Pond

Lone Pasture

N

(Not to Scale)

January

The sun is rising over a landscape chilled by an overnight frost. The skeletal remains of last year's cow parsley glitters with ice crystals forming delicate crowns, each fragile spindle fortified by the cold. Desiccated thistles are transformed into spiny ice sculptures, with twisted and brittle leaves glistening, their wizened teasel heads bowed as the stems no longer have the strength to support them. The low sun is blindingly bright and casts long shadows as I walk across The Park towards the ponds. The last few months have been some of the wettest I can remember, and the farm is sodden, its clay foundations holding onto the water as it settles into the gentle undulations to form pools and channels stretching across the land. The surface of the puddles has iced over, a thin glass window beneath which the muddy grass suffocates and drowns. In the distance, a kestrel is laughing.

Against a pink-tinged sky, the thick hedgerows are sleeping, no signs yet of a spring awakening. Here and there clusters of berries cling like rubies to lichen-coated branches, but many have already been stripped by marauding mobs of winter thrushes. Over the past few years, the diversity and abundance of birds on the farm has acted like a barometer for the health of the land. As the habitats slowly begin to improve, the birds are returning to the farm and the volume of birdsong has audibly increased, along with the variety of voices that contribute to it. This morning, with the landscape deep in its winter hibernation, the birds are waking and the slumbering hedgerow jostles with life. A rowdy gang of goldfinches chatter to one another, perched like baubles on the bare branches at the top of a field maple, and the sad 'seep-seep' of a redwing cuts through a blackbird's melody. Somewhere in the dense, tangled undergrowth a wren scutters, firing out its rattling call at a volume and intensity that belies its diminutive size.

My wellies crunch through the frost and I disturb a woodcock nestled among the grasses and brambles that skirt the bottom of the hedge. Its freckled plumage, stippled with earthy tones of brown and grey had rendered it invisible, and it startles me as it clatters out of the undergrowth, jinking left and right erratically as it escapes potential danger.

I love mornings like these. The cold needles at my cheeks but I'm cosy and warm inside my fleece and woolly hat. I clamber up the mound at the most western edge of the farm, formed from the spoil when we dug the ponds, which provides some moderate elevation in an otherwise flat landscape. I arrive at the top just in time to see a red fox clear the dyke and disappear into a neighbour's field. From here I can see across The Park, over the hedgerows that flank the track and across to Benard's Field and Lone Pasture. Today, the bottom two-thirds of both fields appear to be on fire, as vast pools of frozen water reflect the neon sky. A lone tree, an old ash that has somehow escaped the ravages of ash dieback, is the last remnant of a hedgerow that once ran across both fields, ripped up by the tides of progress and an urgent drive for more efficiency in farming that has characterized the last century. It owes its life, in part, to Jack's brother Tom. Despite the inconvenience and time needed to manoeuvre heavy machinery around isolated trees, he always insisted that the remaining trees peppered across their land, standing lonely and majestic among seas of crops, were to stay. I have no idea why the farmers that took the hedgerow out in the first place decided that the ash was different from the other trees. Perhaps they liked the twisting branches that sprawled and spread out. Perhaps there was a tawny owl nesting deep in its hollow core and they spared it for the sake of the birds. Perhaps they meant to come back and finish the job but never got around to it. The ash sits on a ridge that crosses the land where the fields climb gingerly out of the watery lowland. From here, it's striking how much variation there is in the vegetation that has started to colonize the land. Where we once tried to bully the land into uniform conformity, it is now free to express its own nature and the subtle differences in substrate and soils are reflected in the different plants that thrive there. Self-set copses of birch and sallow yield to coarse sedges and creeping buttercup that fade into a finer sward interspersed with the bare bones of young hawthorn and dog rose sleeping through their first or second winters.

For as long as I can remember, I have found my peace in nature. As a child, I spent hours alone in our small garden. I knew the smell and texture of every leaf. I learned which rocks to turn over to find wood lice and centipedes. I could tell which flowers the earwigs preferred, under which wooden windowsill I would find a butterfly's chrysalis suspended, and where to avoid sitting on the lawn if I didn't want to end up bitten by the red ants that nested in the grass. I knew every bush that housed an old nest and the birds that built them. I marvelled at the feather, mud and moss linings. I crept out after dark to greet a hedgehog that lived under an old yew tree and counted the spots of ladybirds. When I wasn't outside looking at nature, I was inside drawing it. My mum kept hundreds of drawings and paintings that I had done over the years, and it wasn't until I found them after her death years later, that I realized how much my childhood passions had foreshadowed the career I thought I had fallen into by accident and circumstance. Quiet, studious and sometimes a little lonely at school, I won a place at Cambridge to study Zoology and finally found myself among people who shared my intense curiosity for the natural world. I loved every minute and every aspect of my degree. I loved the academic side, reading cutting-edge research that unlocked scientific mysteries; I loved the fieldwork where I would always have a sketch book and pencil with me; and I loved the social side, finally discovering a confidence that had eluded my earlier teens. This newfound confidence, combined with a fiery ambition that had always burned inside me, propelled me towards London after graduating to pursue a shiny and exciting career in the City. I lasted five years before limping back to Lincolnshire, exhausted and homesick.

> For as long as I can remember, I have found my peace in nature. As a child, I spent hours alone in our small garden. I knew the smell and texture of every leaf.

Within a year of coming home, Jack and I were married, had our first child and my mum was diagnosed with terminal cancer. Suddenly everything changed. I needed a job that would fit around a baby and allow me to spend as much time with my mum as possible. I turned back to what I knew best – nature and art. After a few years of trying different ideas, Wrendale Designs in its current form was born. Watercolour illustrations of wildlife, printed on beautiful-quality, sustainably sourced greeting cards was where it started, and within a few years the collection had grown and we were selling home and giftwares all over the world. The opportunity to return our farm to nature felt like the closing of a circle. It was an opportunity to 'give back' to the animals and birds that had always inspired me and my artwork and a deep and primal feeling that this was the right thing to do.

In my forties, I'm haunted by worries that never darkened my youthful thoughts. The world seems a terrifying place. I fear for the future my children will have to face if we fail to address the climate crisis, the collapse of nature that we are careering towards

with alarming certainty, and the chaos that will ensue as a result. A sense of helplessness and frustration with the wanton and careless destruction of nature feeds a despair that is hard to control, but out here the cold air, the birdsong and the sunrise pour a soothing balm over the seething anger that sometimes threatens to overwhelm me.

As the last vestiges of darkness begin to fade, a large, pale bird silently coasts across The Park on broad, rounded wings. A ghost. It glides seemingly weightless across the field, surveying for the smallest rustle that will yield the location of an unlucky field vole or mouse. The slow cadence of its wing beats lifts it over the hedge into Fox Cover before it circles back, low and quiet over the frosty grass. It alights on a fence post where it rests for a while, its watchful eyes coal black studs in its flat, heart-shaped face. Barn owls are perfectly adapted to silently hunt their prey. They have large wings relative to their low body weight (known as low wing loading), which allows them to fly slowly, giving them time to detect prey as they glide along. They even have tiny hooks along the feather at the leading edge of the wing that help to deaden the sound of air hitting it. Although their eyes are adapted to work well in the dark, experiments have shown that barn owls are perfectly capable of catching prey in complete darkness, using sound alone. Their heart-shaped faces direct sound into their ears and they have among the most sensitive hearing of any animal. Before long the owl abandons its perch and disappears over the hedge towards the track. When we built a pole barn a few years ago, we installed high, flat platforms in the eaves for barn owls, and we often find pellets in there from owls and kestrels who also take advantage of its shelter. I wonder if it has gone there to roost now the sun is rising higher in the winter sky. I head back to the house, restored and refreshed. Not a bad way to start the new year.

February

I've always been a morning person – a lark rather than an owl. My
most productive hours are the early ones before anyone else in
the house has stirred. I often wake several hours before the alarm,
my mind immediately flitting to whatever painting I'm working
on. As soon as this happens, I know that sleep won't return and I
totter downstairs in slippers and dressing gown, make a coffee and
head to my work room. This morning, my brain has decided that
I have had enough sleep by 4.30 am and I suddenly have a craving
to be outside. I put on my coat and wellies over my pyjamas and
grab my binoculars. The night has been mild and clear. The moon
is large and full, a milky orb resting on a wisp of migrating cloud.
Pale, white moonlight washes across the landscape and forms long,
eerie shadows. They streak over the familiar surroundings like cold
fingers probing into every crease and fold.

   I walk towards Fox Cover along the track, flanked by abundant
hedgerows and a tangle of brambles. The daytime soundscape is
filled with the melodic song of blackbirds, thrushes and robins,
interspersed with the ubiquitous rattle of Jenny wren. In the dark
it is transformed. A pair of tawny owls duet, the male's fluting
vibrato answered by the female's shrill 'kee-wick'. Little owls are
shouting at one another from their perches in trees nestled along
the hedgerow. The screeches and hoots are suddenly upstaged by
piercing screams. Somehow human and other-worldly at the same
time, the mandrake-like shrieks are shocking in their volume and
intensity. Rounding the corner of Fox Cover, I crouch among the
gnarled roots of an old oak tree and the moonlight betrays the
source of the screaming. It is mating season for foxes and this

unearthly overture is their idea of a love song. A pair are cavorting in the field, flirting and teasing one another. They pounce and play fight like cubs, all part of the courtship ritual that will continue for weeks before mating occurs. Foxes are monogamous and often pair for life. These behaviours help to reinforce their bond, important in foxes as both parents will play an active role in raising their young. They eventually disappear over the bridge into The Park. This pair successfully raised three cubs last year in an earth conveniently excavated for them by a clan of badgers, the two species quite happily rubbing along together.

Across the field, a pair of roe deer are browsing and a badger snuffles for worms. Dozens of rabbits are going about their business and every so often a snipe or a woodcock senses my unwelcome presence and flushes out of the grass. This shadowy nocturnal world is entirely different from its daytime incarnation. Dewy damp thickens the air and an earthy, mossy smell pervades. My skin tingles with a nervous energy as I intrude where I don't belong. During the day, these nocturnal creatures reveal themselves only in tantalizing, fleeting glimpses. They are emboldened by the darkness and this world is theirs. I am a voyeur. I creep back down the track towards the house, exhilarated and inspired.

Later that day I take the same journey down the track towards Fox Cover. The air is filled with the orchestral harmony of songbirds and a green woodpecker yaffles away in the wood. Across the field, a flock of meadow pipits forages for insects, and skylarks have woken up, flinging themselves vertiginously into the air before floating down in full song.

As I cross over the badger sett by the bridge into The Park, I think of them asleep under my feet, waiting for nightfall to reclaim the farm once more.

* * * * *

It has felt like a long winter this year. The thrill of cosy evenings curled up by the fire has long since worn thin and it's a relief to see the first signs of spring emerging. Swathes of snowdrops nodding their elegant heads have appeared in bright clusters and the shoots of daffodils stand straight like little soldiers waiting for their turn to burst into flower.

The weather has been wintry over the past few weeks – a sustained frost followed by several days of strong winds made it difficult for the barn owls to hunt and I'm dismayed to come across the remains of one on the edge of Church Wood. It's the most deadly time of year for juvenile barn owls as vole numbers are at their lowest – around 70 per cent die in their first year and these inexperienced birds struggle the most during severe weather conditions. Even knowing that the odds are stacked against them, it's dreadful to think that there is one less of these beautiful birds on the farm.

The hazels in the wood are bedecked with catkins, dangling from the branches like little lamb's tails. I've come to the hazel copse at the edge of Church Wood to see whether I could find a little magenta-coloured treasure easily missed by an unknowing observer. Sure enough, at the end of each shoot adorned by catkins is a tiny flower with hot pink, spiky stigmas like some kind of punk sea urchin. Hazels are monoecious, meaning that they have separate male and female flowers. Unlike plants that rely on insects to pollinate them, the hazel has no need of showy petals or intoxicating scent to attract the attention of passing pollinators. Instead, each catkin contains more than 200 male flowers that release clouds of pollen into a passing breeze that carries it away to neighbouring hazels where it can pollinate the little pink female flowers.

Beyond the wood, another species is making its presence known. A speckled brown bird, slightly smaller than a starling with a tufty

Tiny magenta flower with spiky petals, beautiful but tinged encased in pink and green

Lime green, yellow, orange

Bare branches decorated with hundreds of catkins in clusters like little caterpillars

Each are made from tessellating flowers

crest upon its head, the skylark looks unassuming until it unveils its superpower. Soaring vertically into the sky before exploding into a cascade of melodious song while suspended in the air, it floats down like a parachute held aloft by the buoyancy of its song alone. Skylarks, once a common sight across farmland, are disappearing rapidly and, along with so many other species, their numbers in free fall. A lover of tussocky grass pastures, we've seen large flocks amassing over the past few weeks and now the birds are pairing up and the males have begun their display. It is thought that the energy needed for these eccentric behaviours is a good indicator of the fitness of the males, helping the discerning females to choose a suitable mate. Creatures of habit, skylarks return to the same area every year, and it's lovely to see such an abundance of them here on the farm showering their liquid warbles down from the sky. It is little wonder that these birds have inspired so much poetry and art and I am deeply saddened that so few people are able to experience their song in depressingly vacant expanses of our countryside.

It's a lovely day to be out sketching and I estimate there are around 80–90 skylarks displaying and filling the air with a continuous stream of mellifluous song. They pause between performances, sitting on the fence line among reed warblers, yellowhammers, chaffinches, stonechats and buntings. I'm totally immersed in my work, peering through my binoculars, every sense stimulated. All too soon, reality beckons with the impending school run drawing closer but I close my book feeling lifted and refreshed, the birdsong still echoing in my head.

March

It's chilly and damp but there are signs everywhere that spring is jostling to take over from winter. Swollen leaf buds adorn bare branches, full of the promise of verdancy just around the corner. Snowdrops are tired and withered after their early exertions while delicate crocuses are enjoying their time in the sun and fresh shoots, bold with the confidence of youth, are emerging everywhere. The hedgerows are already full of birdsong, the melancholy fluting of song thrushes providing a backdrop for the robin's soprano, while a wren loudly demands to be heard.

Over at the sett, the badgers have been indulging in some spring cleaning. Bundles of discarded bedding have been dragged out and abandoned in jumbled piles. It's likely that somewhere underneath my feet the sows are tenderly nursing their newly born cubs who will stay safely tucked away in their subterranean cocoon until April.

Kestrels, defying gravity above the farm, are a common sight. When vole numbers are abundant, a kestrel's territory is relatively small, so it's a promising sign that the farm is able to support several pairs. Apparently untroubled by our presence, a young male kestrel has settled around the house and roosts on a convenient waste pipe that runs above our sitting room window. The result is an impressive, chalky white abstract masterpiece on the window below and a collection of small furry pellets studded with tiny bones. During the day, his favourite perch is at the top of a high wall that marks the boundary between the garden and The Park, an old established grassland. Years of enrichment had resulted in lush grass that could support higher numbers of beef cattle but

the loss of a myriad of delicate and
diverse meadow flowers that were
unable to compete with the vigorous
grass or excessive grazing. Over
the last few years, we have
taken the cattle off the land
and harvested a cut of hay
late each summer to help
remove some fertility
from the soil. It is clear
that the land still holds the
memories of its past life, and in the first spring
that the grazing pressures were lifted we were rewarded
with an explosion of pignut flowers covering the entire
field, lacy little umbellifers that had been waiting patiently
for a chance to bloom. Each year, increasing numbers of flowers
are tentatively emerging, and we are seeing the return of cowslips,
great burnet, ragged robin, viper's bugloss, buttercups and even the
occasional orchid. The area is still dominated by grass and there
is a long way to go but we're slowly coaxing the old meadow to
reawaken. It is the kestrel's preferred hunting ground and this is
where he likes to sit and survey his kingdom. Today, it appears that
something unusual has caught his eye.

Before I see them, I hear the starlings. Hundreds of individual
voices chattering away create a monotone clamour quite unlike
any other sound on the farm. Like some kind of biblical swarm,
the air is suddenly filled with little torpedos that land with a swift
motion on the grass, and the entire garden is eclipsed by the noisy
mob. With frenzied haste, the starlings furiously raid the lawn for
any unsuspecting grubs, all the while maintaining their chaotic
conversations. Iridescent hues shimmer on the ground – purples,
blues, greens and blacks glinting and glimmering in the sunlight.

An unexpected movement by the kestrel on the wall sets into motion a perfectly coordinated chain reaction, accompanied by a whooshing sound like a wave breaking on the shore, as hundreds of wings beat the air in unison. The cloud of birds lifts, waxing and waning like a shimmering shoal of fish, moving to the rhythm of an unseen conductor. I hold my breath as I watch the swirling, swooping shape.

As quickly as they arrived, the starlings have departed. The flock envelops the branches of an oak tree and nearby telegraph wires, where they sit like musical notes on an orchestral score. Starlings are remarkable birds. Famous for their mesmerizing murmurations, which can consist of thousands of individuals, they are incredibly social and are amazing mimics. They can make a huge variety of sounds and captive birds have even learned to imitate human voices. Population declines have meant that starlings are now considered a Red List Threatened Species by the International Union for the Conservation of Nature (IUCN).

Stretching his wings, the kestrel settles back into his vigilant watch over The Park, perhaps relieved that the temporary madness has passed.

* * * * *

This week, a neighbouring farmer invited us to attend the parish council meeting held in the local church. This farmer, well into his eighties, had introduced himself when we moved to the village as 'the self-appointed ragwort police', so we had a fair idea what might be coming.

Before we took our land out of arable production, we gave a great deal of thought to what was the 'right' thing to do with it. Jack's family had farmed in Lincolnshire for generations and we have deep connections with the farming community in our area. The vast majority of the farmers we know care about the countryside and take their responsibilities as stewards of the land seriously. They balance this with the challenges of running an incredibly stressful business and grappling with government directives and incentives as best they can. However, this hasn't stopped biodiversity from collapsing around us as farming techniques have intensified, and it's clear that there needs to be a step change in the way the countryside is managed. Conventional farming can become more nature friendly, and it can continue to exist alongside regimes that support and restore nature and natural processes – the two systems can, and should, operate hand in hand, supporting and benefiting one another. Prime and productive arable farmland is best used to grow food that can be eaten by humans, but where the land is poor and unyielding it can offer far more value to wildlife than to food production. According to DEFRA, 42 per cent of England's farms produce a meagre 2 per cent of the total agricultural output. Our marginal land falls into this category and this underpinned our decision to take it out of cultivation and instead dedicate it to our impoverished wildlife.

However, even if we can agree that the decision to devote our farm to nature is morally and practically sound, the reality of the changing landscape is another hurdle to reconcile. We've tried our best to engage our neighbours with what we are doing on the farm, and almost without exception we have been met with excitement and interest. Many have commented on how much more wildlife they are experiencing in their gardens and how much the volume of birdsong in the hedgerows that border the farm has increased. However, we did know that one or two were not very happy about the changing character of our land as it morphed overnight from hosting golden swathes of uniform crops to taking charge of its own destiny, replete with all the weedy, scrubby messiness that this entails.

In addition to the farmer already mentioned, a gentleman with a garden close to our fields was particularly unhappy. His preference is to keep his large expanse of garden as pristine and immaculate as a bowling green. Not a flower or weed in sight, just a perfect, uniform sea of grass, each blade clipped neatly to a required length, so it's perhaps understandable that he wasn't thrilled about looking out over a wild and messy landscape rather than a tidy monoculture of wheat.

After just a few short years, we recorded 23 different butterfly species on the farm last summer.

Despite this, I wasn't fazed by the prospect of the meeting. I knew that most of the residents of the village were supportive. Galvanized by the results we were already seeing in terms of diversity and abundance of wildlife on the farm, I also went into the meeting with a deep sense that what we were doing was right. I decided to try and weigh the odds in my favour by pitching the meeting as an update to the village on our work at the farm and the results we were already seeing. I talked about the dire state of wildlife in our country. The UK ranks among the most nature-depleted nations globally, falling within the bottom 10 per cent for biodiversity*: 38 million birds have disappeared from our shores in the past 50 years, and we have lost 60 per cent of all insects in the last 20**. Even on our own doorsteps, one of our neighbours is an amateur lepidopterist, and had mentioned to me that when he

*According to research by the Natural History Museum in its Biodiversity Intactness Index, 2020.
**According to research conducted by the RSPB, the British Trust for Ornithology (BTO) and the Wildflower & Wetland Trust (WWT), 2019.

started recording species in the local area 28 years ago, he would regularly note 21 species of butterfly in a year. This has fallen dramatically and now a normal annual count would amount to only 13 different species. After just a few short years, we recorded 23 different butterfly species on the farm last summer. Our surveyor remarked that it is now likely to be one of the best sites in the county for grassland butterflies. I also talked about the 83 different bird species we have recorded, including 17 IUCN Red List species, and the overall increase in abundance we are seeing as habitats regenerate and the land is given a chance to breathe. I felt that I had done a good job in justifying what we were trying to achieve and talked a little about how I hoped that it would ultimately benefit future generations in the local community.

The words were barely out of my mouth when our garden-proud neighbour spat out his disgust that he was now having to spray pesticides on his lawn four times a year compared with twice a year before we stopped spraying our own land. Then the aforementioned farmer chimed in with his opinions on the appalling state of the land, while a neighbour with a house further up the hill complained that she would have to do more weeding as a result of thistle seeds landing in her garden. Despite admitting that what we were doing didn't really affect his farm as he routinely sprayed anyway, the farmer was deeply offended by what he saw as wanton neglect. Throughout his long life, this farmer would have known our land before hedges were pulled up and when hay meadows were bright with flowers and butterflies. In his childhood, the air would have been full of birdsong and he would have farmed alongside species now long gone, such as corncrake and red-backed shrike. Hedgehogs would have been abundant, and bats would have roosted in cavities forged in the ancient oaks that were studded through the hedgerows, before being ripped out in the name of progress. I am so devastated by all of this catastrophic loss and filled with a sense of urgency to protect and restore what is left that I found it incredibly hard to empathize with his objections, but ever the voice of reason, Jack was able to at least attempt to see things from his point of view. In the past, before the routine use of chemical sprays on farms, weed control was necessary to ensure reasonable harvests. Tidy hedgerows and verges were a source of pride. Success has been measured in increasing yield and productivity, and nature has either been framed as an obstacle to be exterminated in order to allow continued progress, or as collateral damage of the same. The 'neatness' epidemic has taken root and it is extremely difficult to change views that are held with such religious fervour.

Understanding the need to work alongside our local community, one early decision that we made was to plant a woodland around the perimeter of the farm to create a 50-metre (160-foot) 'buffer' between ourselves and our neighbours, protecting their land from the spread of unwanted 'weeds'. Ragwort is one such plant, hated and feared in equal measure. Indeed, it is toxic to cattle and horses, but also tastes unpalatable and under normal circumstances it will be avoided by both. It is mainly a problem in hay meadows that are being cut for fodder. In late July, once the flowers have been used by pollinators but before it has turned to seed, we routinely pull all of the ragwort plants from between the young trees in the new woodland. Research has shown that over 99 per cent of ragwort seeds fall within a 36-metre (120-foot) radius of the plant so we feel that is a responsible management policy to stem the spread of ragwort where it is unwanted beyond our borders. Indeed, the total eradication of plants like ragwort would be disastrous for nature and is not mandated by rules surrounding ragwort control – at least 30 species of invertebrate depend on it exclusively. In time, the growing trees in the new woodland will crowd out these plants and it will also act as a windbreak, reducing the spread of wind-blown seeds from thistles, and indeed, as the scrub matures the thistles will cease to be so dominant anyway. Unfortunately, it became clear that our efforts hadn't been enough for a small number of our neighbours.

As we were attacked by these few angry residents with startling ferocity and I did my best to defend our position, the rest of the audience sat in uncomfortable silence. A couple of half-hearted attempts to defend a more relaxed gardening style were batted away by the passionate and very real anger of a small minority. We agreed to redouble our efforts to mitigate the spread of seeds and were asked to return in a year's time to repeat the experience.

I sat in shocked silence for the remainder of the meeting, barely able to hear anything else that was said. As we shuffled out of the church at the end of the night, another neighbour tried to reassure me that not everyone felt that way, but I could barely manage an indecipherable squeak as I tried to hold back the floodgates. Jack and I went to bed in silence that night, my head full of a million things I should have said but wasn't sharp enough to think of at the time and I cried until my pillow was soaked through. Over the next few days, I received several kind messages of support from the village, and Jack bumped into a dog walker who had been at the meeting who hoped that we weren't too upset and said that everyone that he had spoken to, the 'silent majority', were supportive of what we are doing on the farm. I fervently wished that the majority hadn't been quite so silent at the meeting. However, his words helped to reassure me that we weren't quite the pariahs in the local community that we had felt ourselves to be that night.

Still licking my wounds, over the next few days I spend a lot of time out on the farm. I had been waiting impatiently over the past month to see some signs of amphibians on the move. Despite knowing that we didn't usually have any frogspawn in our ponds until mid-March, my social media feed has been full of images of blobs of jelly nestled among vegetation in garden ponds from other parts of the country. Anxious and impatient, I had been making a daily pilgrimage around the perimeter of the ponds, poking around in the margins and coming back disappointed. The morning after the disastrous meeting, I was finally rewarded with the first gelatinous pile of glorious jelly, studded with little black dots. Satisfied at last, I was on my way back to the house when something else caught my eye. Swollen by recent rainfall, one of the ponds was spilling out onto the grassy bank, and there among the drowning vegetation, a toad orgy was taking place. Everywhere I looked, pairs of toads had coupled up, the smaller males hitching a ride on the backs of the larger females. A symphony of olive greens, yellow ochres and browns, the warty texture of the toads blended perfectly with the grasses and plants that soften the transition between land

and water. Stretching out within the foliage were strings of toad spawn, formed in ribbons rather than clumps like the frogspawn.

After dark, I slip on my wellies and coat and quietly head over to the pond again. It is a dark night and I can't see a thing, but it doesn't matter because the night air is filled with the sound of frogs and toads singing to one another. The percussive rattling of the frogs vibrating from deep in their throats provides the backdrop to the chirping toads. Walking back to the house I think of the new life that the ponds are harbouring and start to feel a little better.

* * * * *

The daffodils have finally erupted into flower. Like molten sunshine, trumpets and stars illuminate grass verges signalling that spring has arrived in all its glory. Unfortunately, the weather has largely not received the message and over the past few days the poor daffodils have been bruised and buffeted by the wind. Resilient and determined, they are standing tall in the sunshine today, despite having spent their early days mainly horizontal.

The blackthorn has also awoken from hibernation, and too impatient to wait for its leaves, the long spines and bare branches are adorned with thousands of pale flowers. The blossoms release an intoxicating perfume and several bees amble sleepily among the flowers, their bodies dusted with pollen. The spines of blackthorn are surprisingly vicious. Up to 10 centimetres (4 inches) long, they are a relic of a distant past when large, wild herbivores roamed our countryside and the blackthorn needed weapons to defend itself.

Overhead, lapwings cartwheel and tumble around on broad, round wings, their 'pee-wit' call transmitting across the sky like someone tuning in an old radio. The males are displaying and the patchwork of wet grassland across the farm will provide them with the habitat they need to raise their chicks.

At the ponds, a small flock of greylags plus an unexpected white goose poke around in the grass. This same group of birds has returned every winter and it seems that the domestic white goose has at some point decided that it prefers the company of its wild cousins. While the greylags retain an innate nervousness, noisily defying gravity to transport their great heft to safety when disturbed, 'Whitey' as he has imaginatively been christened, carries on his business without a second glance. I hope that his strident confidence won't become his undoing one day. A pair of shelducks is enjoying a morning swim, and in a few grassy patches along the edges of the pond, an iridescence reflecting off the surface is evidence of more wading birds. Preen oil, produced from a gland beneath their tails and combed through their feathers, gives the birds a waterproof coating and it is traces of this oil that float on the surface at the margins of the pond. Fortunately, the ducks haven't yet discovered the mounds of jelly nestled among the vegetation and the frogspawn has already started to develop, little commas now instead of full stops at the centre of each globule.

Satisfied and heartened by the early spring sunshine, I head home along the track. Halfway down, I am alerted by the high-pitched, rattling purr of a long-tailed tit. I pause to watch a pair of them busily darting in and out of the tangle of brambles underneath the hedge. There, cocooned within the briars like Sleeping Beauty's castle, is a treasure worthy of the most magical fairy tale – a large oval nest constructed from blue-green lichens, woven together with the silk of spider webs. Long-tailed tits are among my very favourite birds. I love their fluffy round bodies and impossibly long tails, their gregarious nature and excitable chatter. Unfortunately, the majority of long-tailed tit nests fail due to predation by crows, jays, stoats and domestic cats, despite their artistic efforts to build a well-camouflaged nest. Unlike most other small birds, rather than attempting to rebuild or construct a second nest, long-tailed tits sacrifice their own breeding success and lend their efforts to another pair, usually consisting of a close relative. This cooperation greatly increases the birds' chances of successfully raising a brood of chicks and the helpers gain brood-rearing experience as well as contributing to the propagation of their own genes by helping their relatives. The brambles still look bare, their branches adorned with leaf buds that are yet to unfurl and I go to bed that night willing them to grow quicker and hide the nest within their leafy tangles.

* * * * *

We've been away for a week and in that short space of time the countryside has undergone a metamorphosis. The blackthorn hedgerows lining the fields billow like white clouds and where we left bare branches a week ago, fresh green leaves are appearing on the hawthorn. The wild cherry trees are clothed in exuberant blossoms, more showy and extravagant than the blackthorn, and the sweet fragrance of wild garlic fills the air at the edge of the wood. The cherry trees appear to be singing, a loud, resonant hum that settles somewhere deep inside my chest as the bees travel from flower to flower with new urgency. Dainty little chiffchaffs have returned from southern Europe and Africa and call out their name over and over in a rhythmical cadence. A busy pair has made a nest at the base of a bramble patch, verdant vegetation concealing their treasures, and willow warblers are singing their hearts out from the sallow. Visually, these two birds look incredibly similar. Expert birders confidently point to the shade of their slender little legs, or the tone of their buff-coloured belly, but in isolation I still find it difficult to tell the difference until you hear their song. The willow warbler's repeating phrase sounds like tinkling notes cascading down a tiny waterfall.

Anxiously, I head down the track to check on the long-tailed tits and am relieved to see them busying themselves in the hedgerow, and their beautiful lichen nest still intact. Over at the pond, empty globules of jelly no longer house their precious charges and it lies in opaque, abandoned clumps like flaccid balloons. Little tadpoles wriggle around in shallow pools formed among the wet vegetation, and the surface of the water is alive with dancing insects that create cascades of tiny ripples. The toad spawn has also shed its tadpoles and they cling to one another in a huge black mass, each individual a dense little rectangle, still solid and unformed in comparison with the elegant frog tadpoles beating their gossamer tails.

Two large hares tear across the field, possessed by the madness that famously occupies them at this time of year, and I keep coming across little tufts of disembodied fur that have been sent flying during their scrappy boxing matches.

In the warmer wet weather, the grass has started to grow again, and the sward is a mixture of dried hay intermingled with fresh shoots. We took a cut of grass from The Park field in late summer last year to reduce the fertility of the soil, which favours the growth of wild flowers and helps to weaken the thuggish grasses. The late summer cut left it enough time to recover sufficiently to provide the perfect over-wintering habitat for voles. Although we rarely catch sight of these stout little rodents, there is evidence of them all over the farm. Perfectly round holes around 2.5 centimetres (1 inch) in diameter appear to be woven delicately into the thatch of grass. In The Park, there must be on average one of these holes every square metre. They are portals to a complex network of passageways existing in the liminal space between the earth and the sky. This is the world of the field vole. Life is fast and short for these enterprising rodents. In nests made from shredded grasses, a female can produce up to six litters of eight young in a single year, but population sizes boom and bust over a three- to four-year cycle. Since we stopped cultivating our land, the vole numbers that the habitat can support has increased dramatically and we have seen the evidence for this in the appearance of predators that rely on voles as a vital food source. Where the skies above a ploughed field were once as barren and empty as the land beneath them, barn and tawny owls now glide, their acute sense of hearing detecting any small movement from the voles in their burrows. Kestrels hover, their heads miraculously still before dive-bombing any unfortunate vole careless enough to be detected. Foxes pounce energetically into the grass, catching their prey unawares. Marsh harriers occasionally visit over winter and we currently have another resident on the farm that we had never seen before this year. Short-eared owls are birds of both the sky and the earth. Unlike barn and tawny owls, which prefer to roost high up in the trees or on ledges safety tucked away in the corners of barns, short-eared owls roost and nest on the ground, favouring the rough grassland and scrubby pasture that supports a large vole population. We had brief glimpses of a short-eared owl on the farm several times over the winter. The first time, we surprised one another as I inadvertently disturbed its grassy roost and it burst out indignantly in a flurry before plopping down again further away. Today, as the sun begins to dip towards the horizon, it is hunting over Fox Cover, briefly perching on a fence post before gliding low over the thatch. It is as pale as the grass but each feather is tattooed with jet black striations. Its flat face is punctuated by eyes the colour of egg yolk surrounded by thick kohl eyeliner. Its wings are broad like those of a barn owl but longer, giving it a more languorous, fluid flight, powered by measured, metronomic pulses. Occasionally, it banks like a spitfire, the flat face parallel with the ground when, in a whip-fast motion, it plunges its feet armed with deadly talons into the sward, its long wings collapsing like a folding umbrella. For the millionth time I'm reminded of why we are doing this. And it feels good.

Using (a host of feather markings)

Clear strong markings well defined.

Striking yellow eyes golden luminescent + surrounded by jet black

Huge Wingspan

April

The weather in our country is fickle and unpredictable. In the years that Jack was farming, the state of the weather was a constant source of anxiety. Even now as we walk across a sodden field, several inches deep in water, Jack is shaking his head and muttering to himself 'imagine trying to drill into this', his broken nights of worrying about when the land would be dry enough to get onto with machinery still haunting him. As we increasingly feel the impact of climate change, the weather seems to be even more difficult to predict.

Two years ago, Jack and I embarked on the mammoth project of planting 27,000 trees around the perimeter of the farm. Planting, as opposed to waiting for natural regeneration to populate the land with trees, can be a divisive subject. There is a strong argument that artificially introducing even a native mix of trees can change the character of an area and that the earth itself knows best what will thrive in the very specific conditions it can provide. There has also been a change of thinking in recent years regarding closed canopy woodland. The perceived wisdom that Britain was once cloaked from head to foot in dense woodland has been challenged and a more dynamic picture has emerged. With large grazing herbivores shaping the landscape before humans arrived on the scene, it is more likely that wood pasture was the dominant habitat – a complex and constantly changing system that incorporates a mosaic of scrub, open grassland, small copses and scattered trees. You only have to look at an open grown oak, branches twisting and sprawling, clothed in leaves from the crown to the lowest branch that touches the earth, and compare this with a wood-grown oak, die-straight as it competes with its neighbours for light, having given up on its lower branches, with a tiny cap of leaves at the top, to understand that this is a tree that enjoys its solitude. We probably need to rethink our definitions when it comes to 'woodland' and certainly shift away from rows of densely packed trees in favour of a more diverse and complex habitat. Tree guards and deer fencing are another tricky issue – we are constantly picking up bits of plastic from the wood that was planted with tree guards 30 years ago – it seems to be a never-ending job, and no one wants to see the countryside littered with the remnants of plastic tree guards.

On the other hand, our land has been changed beyond recognition after centuries of farming, and the original seed bank is long since depleted. In addition, without apex predators to keep deer numbers in check, it is much harder for young saplings to thrive under the constant grazing pressure that they exert. We see evidence of this all over the farm. After only a couple of years, scrub is starting to appear – wild roses, hawthorn and blackthorn, unleashed from the confines of the hedgerow, are enjoying a newfound freedom, and sallow, a fast-growing willow that specializes in colonizing barren land, is popping up everywhere. Little oak saplings, their seeds likely cached away and forgotten by jays, optimistically offer up their fresh leaves to the sun only to be nibbled down to the ground by browsing deer. Strings of ragged bark hang limply from young tree stems that have been gnawed by browsing teeth.

We also had the practical need to create a buffer between our land and that of our neighbours, and we reasoned that planting around the perimeter of the farm would maximize the amount of 'woodland edge'. With access to light and warmth, the transitional zone between the edge of a wood and another habitat such as a meadow is a species-rich, diverse and dynamic habitat that often contains most of the life in a wood, perhaps because it offers the conditions most similar to those found in wood pasture. After careful consideration, we decided to go ahead with the planting, and this was when we had the first indication that some of our neighbours weren't going to be thrilled about our plans for the farm.

We had consulted with the Forestry Commission regarding the woodland and applied for a woodland creation grant to cover the cost of establishing the trees. As part of the grant terms, we were obliged to inform the local community of the plans. Unfortunately, the land agent jumped the gun and sent a letter to the parish council before we had a chance to lay out our plans in person and to say it didn't go down well in some quarters is an understatement. Suffice to say, the same individuals who don't like thistles and ragwort were also less than keen about woodland being planted on the farm. I think this was the moment they realized we weren't going to farm the land conventionally, and the idea of it reverting to a more wild and unruly state deeply offended them. We received a formal letter asking us to reconsider our plans, stating that wildlife was currently thriving on the farm, that planting a woodland would harm rather than help wildlife, that crops capture more carbon than forestry and that receiving funding to plant trees when it could be given to farmers was, in their opinion, immoral. In addition to this, we also received a request to leave things as they were in the form of a short poem. The author was anonymous but their work is currently framed on the wall of our downstairs loo. Their general feeling was that they liked the village as it was and didn't want any change.

This reaction took us by surprise. We really didn't think that planting trees would be controversial, and ironically, one of the reasons we were doing it was in anticipation of concerns from these very same people relating to the spread of 'weed' seeds. Neither Jack nor myself are very good with confrontation. Jack has the peacemaker tendencies of a typical middle child and avoids conflict at all costs, and while I will square up for a fight more readily, I hate the idea of people disliking me and have a strong need to feel that I am doing the right thing morally. The thought that people were criticizing us for planting trees was incredibly uncomfortable. We were able to answer each point in the letter calmly and scientifically and made some concessions such as planting smaller species closer to the edge of the wood to limit any shading. This seemed to put the matter to rest (at least that was the last we heard of it) and we continued with our plans.

In January 2021, 27,000 trees of 13 native species were delivered to the farm. To mimic wood pasture as closely as possible, and to maximize the value to wildlife, we wanted our woodland to include sunny glades opening up into warm, sheltered pockets, messy scrubby edges and space for giant oaks to unfurl into. To create this natural effect, we had decided to plant every one of the trees by hand rather than relying on machinery which would have planted them in straight rows. Not for the first or last time, we were met with the overwhelming feeling that we had bitten off more than we could chew when hundreds of pallets were delivered to the farm. Jack had calculated how long he thought it would take to plant the trees and he had vastly underestimated it. Planting a sapling into crumbly, loamy soil that forms a neat hole with the spade and tumbles back in to caress the tender roots of the young tree is one thing. Planting it into sticky, wet clay that clings to your boots and spade in great, claggy chunks, weighing it down and dulling it is quite another. A few weeks into the planting, we were exhausted and utterly fed up. The weather was cold and wet and the whole experience was pretty miserable. We decided to call in some help:

there were a couple of days when volunteers from Wrendale came to help us, and we roped in friends who kindly gave their time in return for a cold beer and some pizza. With a long way still to go, I tentatively enquired on the village Facebook page whether there would be interest in a tree planting day. The response was overwhelming and on a (mercifully) sunny Sunday in early March, 30 of our neighbours came to help us. It was a fantastic day, helped no doubt by the lovely weather and there was a real sense of community as we shared stories, sandwiches and spades.

As bad luck would have it, having planted through a wet and soggy winter, we were hit with an incredibly dry April and no amount of staring at the sky wishing for rain made any difference at all. As is the wont of our land, it baked hard, very quickly forming deep crevices. The young saplings hadn't had the chance to put down roots to access water deep in the ground and many didn't survive. After hundreds of hours of back-breaking work planting the trees, we were devastated to see that so many of them were reduced to dry twigs. The following year there was a small glimmer of hope – many of the trees that we had given up on had in fact retained a spark of life within them and had sent out new shoots from the base despite having abandoned the original stem. The following summer we were faced with apocalyptic 40-degree-Celsius heat and many of the wild cherries that had got away well withered and died, exhausted by the extreme temperatures. The high failure rate of planted woodland is another argument for leaving it to nature.

Last winter, we replaced many of the trees that had died and then there was little we could do but wait and see how the spring weather unfolded. So far, in contrast with the parched April of two years ago, this one has been cool and wet and I'm hopeful that this time round the rain will provide enough nourishment for the tender saplings to thrive.

I take a walk this evening across the farm to the ponds. True to form, the weather is cold and wet and I'm starting to question my need to be outside as the wind drives the raindrops into my face like painful little darts. Beneath my feet the grass is sodden, squelching softly under my weight. At times, my wellies are deep under water. Lonely cowslips valiantly persevere, clusters of buttery flowers nodding in the wind, straining the slender stems that stand above a velvety rosette of green. My approach is announced by a soft honking and an indignant ruffling of feathers that sends a torrent of ripples strafing across the surface of the water. I stop in my tracks, not wanting to disturb the geese that had settled around the pond, when a movement catches my eye. On a grassy island in the middle of one of the ponds, a female mallard is settling into the vegetation with a clutch of fluffy brown and yellow ducklings that can't be more than a few days old. They nestle in around her and seem to

melt into her feathers, shielding themselves from the rain and wind. In turn, the long vegetation envelops them all in its protective embrace. Her mottled brown markings are echoed in the shades of the reedy grasses around her and they disappear into the landscape as though they had never been there at all. I back away and trudge through the driving rain to the house and fervently hope that the weather improves. I have some packing to do.

One of the many unexpected delights of the path we have taken with the farm is the connection we have made with many people that we would never otherwise have met. Clever people, passionate about nature restoration. Brave people, who take risks and push against the tide, undeterred by the criticism and abuse they sometimes receive as a result of their convictions. People who share our values and passion and who have made us feel part of a community. We are learning all the time and are constantly looking for advice and trying to absorb the skills and knowledge of others who have far more experience than us. We have decided to take a trip to Cornwall tomorrow to visit Woodland Valley Farm, a third-generation farm that has been organic since 2002, run by Chris Jones, his wife Janet and their daughter Felicity. Passionate about developing a farming system that allows nature to flourish alongside it, Chris and Janet are pioneers, and their beautiful farm nestled into a Cornish valley is inspirational. In 2017, Chris and Janet welcomed a new species to their land, and these animals are the reason for our visit. After an absence of over 400 years, Woodland Valley Farm welcomed a pair of beavers back to Cornwall.

* * * * *

We arrive on the south coast after long hours of claustrophobic travelling and I am impatient to get outside, stretch my legs and fill my lungs with cold, fresh air. There are many familiar voices here – skylarks blast out their song into the buffeting wind, wrens rattle away in the hedgerows and a male linnet, blushing crimson in his seasonal garb, trills melodiously as he flutters from branch to branch. The illusion of familiarity is overlaid onto a landscape altogether wilder and edgier than the one I'm used to in Lincolnshire. Rhythmical undulations give way to sudden, gnarled eruptions of ancient rock littered with fragments of vegetation that eke out a living in creases and crevices. Where the land plunges away vertiginously and the plants are safe from the incessant nibbling of grazers they become braver and a botanical arms race rages in slow motion. Gorse glows like embers burning on the hillside and drifts of blue spring squill hunker down and point their faces to the sun as sea thrift cloaks the hillsides in blush pink.

It's a calm day despite the salty wind that chases around the clifftops. The sea is a sleeping dragon breathing steadily. Every so often she flexes her rippling muscles sending showers of spray over the rocks, a show of the latent power barely concealed beneath her surface and ready to be unleashed if anyone dares to anger her.

My binoculars are practically glued to my eyes as I take in all of the birdlife that has evolved to take advantage of the riches that the coastal habitat has to offer. Gannets circle gracefully before firing like bullets into the water. Hitting the surface at up to 100 kilometres (60 miles) per hour, they have evolved a suite of adaptations to ensure

fulmar pair nestled on rocky ledge

Off white, grey snowy white. Dark eyes

Superficially gull like but head and beak shape is distinct

they are able to survive the impact. As well as internal nostrils that can be closed during the dive, they have developed the avian equivalent of airbags – pockets of air linked to their respiratory systems that help to cushion the blow. Along the coast, a colony of fulmars nestles precariously into narrow ledges on the cliff face and a pair are displaying to one another, their heads bobbing up and down before enthusiastically shaking their beaks. Almost gull-like in appearance, fulmars are more closely related to albatrosses and form lifelong pairs. Displaying like this helps to reinforce their bond. The name 'fulmar' comes from old Norse meaning 'foul gull' and refers to another trick in their repertoire – their regurgitation reflex has evolved into a predatory defence mechanism. If threatened, the fulmar will spray out a cocktail of foul-smelling oils that stick to the intruder's feathers, hindering its ability to fly, which can be fatal.

Closer to the surface of the water, busy little guillemots whizz by, their wings beating furiously as a barrelling seal bobs up and down lazily, as though exhausted just by watching them. My favourite spectacle of the day came a little later as we followed the jagged coastal path along its peaks and troughs to a rocky outcrop. Hundreds of travellers have arrived on our shores and have found themselves here in Cornwall. Sleek as arrows, swallows whirl and circle above our heads. There are sand martins and house martins too and together they perform a wild and intricate aerial ballet as they dart in wide arcs across the expansive Cornish sky. It is incredible to think that these birds have endured a perilous journey of 10,000 kilometres (6,000 miles) over land, desert and sea to reach this shoreline. The scene is joyous and we all stand in awe as we watch them swoop and swirl. I wonder whether our swallows will have returned home to Lincolnshire by the time we are back – I've seen a few over the farm, but so far no sign of the birds that come and nest in our barns, and I've been anxious about whether they made the long journey successfully. The thought of a summer without seeing their familiar silhouettes gracefully dancing across the sky is chilling.

* * * * *

Away from the coast, wild hedgerows spill over dry stone walls that are thick with moss as though the landscape is slowly resorbing them and claiming them back as its own. In deep river valleys, lush vegetation glistens with water droplets. Mosses wrap themselves around trees like velvet and ferns grow on branches high up in the canopy. The river muddles along over a pebbly bed, tumbling and tripping over rocks and wind-fallen branches. It sparkles in dappled green sunlight as low boughs cautiously dip their leaves into the cool flow. Dippers nesting along the river perch on emergent stones, bobbing up and down in the curious fashion that earned them their name, before disappearing into the water and reemerging with fat caddisfly larvae. The reason for the repetitive dance is one of nature's mysteries that we've not yet managed to unravel: one theory is that seeing prey from more than one angle helps them to precisely locate it; another is that it allows them to communicate with one another without having to compete with the sound of the gurgling water. For now, the secret is not ours to know. The occasional flash of iridescent blue is the only glimpse we manage to get of kingfishers as they busily hunt fish to feed their own hungry chicks.

Intent upon experiencing as many different habitats as possible over our few short days in Cornwall, we spend some time in a

bird hide at a wetland managed by the RSPB. A whole new cast of characters plays upon this stage and the ponds and scrapes teem with life. Curlews prod and poke their long, curved beaks into the shallow, muddy shores while mallards dive for tasty morsels, their white bottoms and curled tails thrust into the air before they re-emerge, droplets of water rolling off their oiled feathers. Mute swans land on the water with a grace that defies their enormous mass, their feet skimming the surface and upsetting the calm.

With no warning, a whole flock of godwits that had been hidden among a bed of rushes suddenly lifts in unison, murmurating as they orient themselves before making a hasty exit. They are followed by a gang of teal that fly off noisily and there is a flurry of activity among the reeds. Our dull senses had failed to detect the arrival of a dangerous predator. We scan the sky for the source of this sudden panic and eventually we spy what the wetland residents had sensed long before we had. A marsh harrier slides across the sky on broad wings. It circles overhead before locking onto a target. A little moorhen is stranded alone in the middle of a vast expanse of water. Furiously paddling, it makes frustratingly slow progress as the marsh harrier sweeps ominously overhead. Meanwhile, a pair of lapwings that no doubt has a vulnerable clutch of chicks hidden somewhere among the grasses begins to mob the harrier, swooping at it and crying out with electronic-sounding distress calls. This seems to cause the harrier little more than mild irritation and it takes a swift attempt at the moorhen, plunging towards it, talons first. With impeccable timing, the moorhen dives under water just as the harrier breaks the surface and it is unable to grasp hold of the moorhen. Ignoring the persistent bothering of the lapwings, the harrier circles round and takes another dive. Once again, the moorhen bobs under the surface of the water just in time to avoid the deadly grasp. We all hold our breath as the moorhen desperately tries to reach the edge of the pond and the harrier has a third attempt. This time, it manages to claim a tenuous grip on the little bird, but it is not enough and the moorhen is lifted by barely a couple of centimetres before slipping back into the water. Fourth and fifth attempts are also unsuccessful and we are mesmerized by the dramatic scene that is unfolding before us. Eventually, the marsh harrier has had enough and sulkily drops down onto the bank to preen its feathers nonchalantly. The lucky moorhen makes it to the side and disappears into the vegetation, seemingly unruffled by such a close encounter with its own mortality.

The next stop on our journey is Woodland Valley Farm, the real reason for our trip. We are given a warm welcome by Janet and she proudly gives us a tour. She introduces us to her cattle that are mob grazed around the fields, a technique of intensively grazing small areas over short periods of time and continuously moving them around the farm giving the grazed areas a chance to recover. It is thought that this technique better mimics natural grazing habits of herds and it has been shown to promote better soil health and water-holding capacity, increased biodiversity, healthier cattle and lower costs. We are taken through a fragment of ancient woodland clinging to a steep valley side that has survived intact while others were felled by neighbours, tempted by the post-war incentives to plough up every piece of available land. Gnarly giants emerge from a soft blue carpet of bluebells and white wood anemones gleam like stars reflected from a clear night sky. The distant drumming of woodpeckers provides a percussive back note to the robin's soprano and the blackcap's soulful alto.

As evening approaches, it is finally time to see what we have come all this way for. In 2017, beavers were reintroduced here into a 2-hectare (5-acre) enclosure in a small area of woodland with a little stream running through it. In a short space of time, the beavers have transformed the landscape. Native to Britain but hunted to extinction over 400 years ago, the beaver is a keystone species. Its activities engineer the ecosystem, creating complex habitats for numerous other species. Chris and Janet have experienced this first hand. Within a few short years, the beavers have built a total of eight dams, which have transformed the single channel into six new ponds and four meandering rivulets that now pass through the site. The beaver-engineered system is far more dynamic and complex than what was there previously; the transition from land to water fluid and mercurial. In periods of drought, water is retained. This is important for Chris, who now has an irrigation source when the rest of the land is parched and thirsty. The system of dams has been shown to improve water quality – in one test, researchers from Cambridge University found an 80 per cent drop in nitrates across the site, buffered by the beaver-dam filtration system. Silt is also caught up in the dams that would otherwise have washed into the sea, clogging up oyster beds and degrading the coastal habitat. The number of dragonfly and damselfly species has more than tripled since the beavers have been there. There are eleven new bird species using the site, and an incredible eleven species of bat have been recorded, where previously there were only four or five. Coppiced willow that grows alongside the water, gnawed into pencil-like points, has vigorously sent out young shoots and the gaps that have been punched into the woodland canopy allow sunlight to flood in, transforming the vegetation and infusing it with life.

The stream passing through Woodland Valley was formerly able to support small numbers of little trout and bullheads. The trout that now inhabit the smaller beaver ponds are twice the size, and in the largest pond they are eight times bigger than those measured in the original stream. Importantly, the pools are full of fry; the system is able to support spawning and with more food and shelter, the fish are thriving. The complex system provides routes past the dams, and in times of high rainfall, Chris is in no doubt that the beaver dams would provide no obstacle for migratory fish – fish that evolved alongside beavers after all. The other major service that Woodland Valley is providing to their local community is helping to reduce the risk of flooding downstream. Exeter University have been monitoring the water flowing through the site, and they found that the flood peak now takes two hours to pass through. It previously took ten minutes for the flood waters to rush down the channel, contributing to flooding in the local village when combined with other floodwater hurtling down canalized streams and dredged rivers. For many millions of years, beavers shaped our landscapes, and their removal must have had catastrophic effects on the wildlife that relied upon the habitat that they created.

As the light fades, we sit quietly by the side of the pond to see if we can catch a glimpse of one of these nocturnal animals, and before long a leathery brown nose appears in the water, a long wake streaming behind it as it glides across the water. A large rodent hauls itself out of the pool and cautiously sniffs the air. Rotund and hairy with large, webbed feet and a flat paddle of a tail, the beaver pauses to scratch its belly before plopping back into the water and swimming off. As the darkness swallows the remaining light, we head out and leave the beavers in peace. Inspired by what we've seen, our heads are full of ideas and plans for what might be possible at home.

In the morning, we head back to Lincolnshire. The landscape ebbs and flows, moulding and changing as we travel north, finally opening up into the huge expansive fields bordered by neatly clipped hedges that we are more familiar with. The bread basket of England, Lincolnshire's relative flatness lends itself to efficient farming practices. The silty soils of south Lincolnshire are nutrient-rich and productive, while the loamy, free draining soils of the gently rolling Wolds are kind and easy to work. Finally, we turn down our lane and head downhill into our valley, where the difficult clay, reclaimed from the marshes, has always been resistant to conform to what has been demanded of it. Tucked away down here, the hedgerows billow, untroubled by the flail, and the verges sing with wild flowers. I am home, and I am so grateful for our wild untidiness.

* * * * *

Today I came across a book in a box of my mother's belongings that I had put aside to sort out another time. The painful task of sorting through a lifetime's worth of possessions must have become overwhelming and this box had languished for another decade before I discovered it again at the back of a dusty cupboard. The book is a small hardback with the spine hanging off. Its pages are yellowed and wavy, having been assaulted by rain showers and probably the occasional splash of tea from a camping mug. The book is *A Field Guide to the British Countryside* by Alfred Leutscher, published the year I was born. Holding it in my hand and feeling its comforting weight, I am instantly transported back to my childhood. The cover features a woodland scene, shafts of sunlight streaming through the canopy to illuminate the leaf-strewn woodland floor. A grey squirrel munches on an acorn and a wren perches on a twig. Although the book belonged to my parents, at some point I had clearly decided to claim it as my own, as my name is etched in pencil on the inside cover, and the pages are decorated with my childish notes, detailing when and where I spotted various animals or birds. The illustrations inside it are beautiful, and each entry is full of fascinating natural history, so much warmer and more insightful than most of the nature guides sitting on my own bookshelf today. Many hours of my childhood were lost poring over this book. I wanted to learn it all, to absorb every fact and to know every insect, bird, plant and fungus by heart. I'm not sure whether this book was a symptom or cause of my feverish obsession with wild things but the sight of its cover has filled me with that odd feeling of sad, comforting nostalgia.

My mum was 56 when she was diagnosed with terminal pancreatic cancer, seven days before I gave birth to my first daughter, Amelia. Coming to terms with the loss of my own mother just as I became a mother myself was devastating. The hard-worn clichés never prepare you for the overwhelming love you feel for your child, but no one told me that it also forces you to see your relationship with your own parents through a different lens, shifting the perspective of every conversation, conflict and sacrifice. I was lucky to have wonderful, supportive parents. My mum was funny, kind, clever, unselfish and endlessly encouraging. We children were her life's work and she devoted herself to us at the expense of her own ambitions and desires. I knew that she loved us, but it wasn't until I had Amelia and was shaken by a primal, violent love for her that I understood how my mum felt about me. This awakening opened a new chapter in our relationship just as it was about to end.

My mum was at her happiest in nature. Her family has Romany roots and her family tree is littered with artists and musicians. She was related to the famous Lincolnshire poacher, Kenzie Thorpe, a wildfowler turned naturalist who painted beautiful scenes of the Lincolnshire marshes and the birds that lived there. She felt a particular affinity with woodland and would often take my brother, my sister and me to the local Twigmoor Woods, a fragment of old woodland, carpeted with bluebells in May and alive with birdsong all year long. We would spend hours there hunting for treasures among twisted, moss-laden roots and imagining fairies dancing among toadstools that sprouted in the damp, dense leaf litter. She took us hunting for tiny star-shaped fossils in a hidden stream that trickled through mossy boulders and thick vegetation near Alkborough, reminiscing about her own childhood memories of spending summers here visiting her Aunt Doll. She and my dad took us rock-pooling along the coast, and I delighted in finding crabs, urchins and starfish alongside cone-shaped limpets and barnacles welded to the salty rocks. I was so lucky to have parents who gave me a glimpse of wildness and encouraged my love of the natural world. As I close the book and slide it on to my bookshelf, I wonder for the millionth time what she would have thought of what we are doing on the farm. I wish more than anything that we could take a walk together and I could show her how things are changing and talk through our hopes and plans for the land.

> I was so lucky to have parents who gave me a glimpse of wildness and encouraged my love of the natural world.

The days are now starting to stretch out, the night receding like a tide to reveal those precious extra hours that smoulder in a dusky half-light. It's a gorgeously mild evening and feeling a little sad and reflective, I decide to take a solitary walk to the place in one of our newly planted woodlands where a pair of grasshopper warblers have been heard singing. The wet spring has done wonders for the sapling trees this year. In particular, the Village Wood, which stands on slightly higher ground, is romping away. Oaks and limes, black poplar and alder now stand almost 2.5 metres (8 foot) tall, wreathed in a halo of fresh green leaves, their tender stems thickening. Around the trees, a patchwork of scrub has begun to develop. Brambles, wild roses and young hawthorns weave their way across the woodland floor, enriching the immature habitat. The grasshopper warbler is a summer migrant from Africa that loves a scrubby environment, scampering like a little mouse among rough grassland and new plantations, so we were excited to learn that its insect-like trills had been heard in the wood at the top of the farm.

It has been raining all day, but the temperatures have been creeping up. Water evaporating away from the ground has made the air feel warm and humid, thick with blossomy perfumes that diffuse from the hedgerows. Across the field in the distance, two pairs of nesting lapwings lift into the air, calling and crying as they tumble and wheel over the sky. Jack remembers his dad pointing out lapwings on the farm to him when he was young, and they have long been a treasured symbol of the countryside. They are known as 'pee-wits' to country folk, an onomatopoeic attempt at describing the bizarre sound they make, quite unlike any other bird I've ever heard, and in all honesty, quite unlike a bird at all. They caper across the sky on broad dark wings rounded at the ends, each beat revealing a flash of white. A closer look through the binoculars reveals a stylish crest licking away from its head, and a rainbow of colours glistening like a pool of oil where a cursory glance may have tricked you into thinking they were simply black. The usual depressing story of habitat loss and declining numbers follows them around like a cloud. The remaining population limps through another breeding season, degraded habitat making them increasingly vulnerable to predation. This is the first time lapwings have returned to the farm to breed for many years and somewhere among the grass pastures at the top end of Benard's Field, we are sure that four pairs of indomitable parents are caring for clutches of outrageously cute, stripy, fluffy chicks. I am giving the whole area a wide berth until I'm sure that they have fledged – it's simply not worth inadvertently risking their breeding success.

I reach the wood and wander through, revelling in the satisfaction of the trees finally getting away and poke through the grass to spot caterpillars, slugs and snails feasting on a smorgasbord of leaves and undergrowth. A whole host of warblers are singing, from chiffchaffs to willow warblers, whitethroats to blackcaps. A pair of sedge warblers serenade one another at the edge of the wood, but this evening there is no sign of the distinctive trilling of the grasshopper warbler. I hang around for another half an hour, but the light is rapidly fading, so I begin the trek home. The whole farm takes on the purple hue of twilight and there is a sense of transition, a changing of the guard. The hedgerows fall silent as blackbirds and thrushes roost for the night and the fluttering of feathered wings is replaced by the delicate flickers of little pipistrelles just awoken from their winter hibernation. A white barn owl floats over the surface of the field like a ghost, and closer to the house I can hear the mewing of a little owl. A female roe deer barks loudly close by. Hidden by trees, her disembodied bark is a little disconcerting and I quicken my pace. A thick mist is now rising from the ground, obscuring and concealing as it meets the darkening sky, enveloping the last glow of soft light like a closing book.

May

Like clockwork, the hawthorn flies have emerged and the air around the hedgerows is filled with their hairy black bodies. They drift around like a dark thundercloud, long legs dangling beneath them. The males have enormous eyes, shaped by evolution to help them to locate the females that emerge slightly later. The hawthorn fly is also known as the St Mark's fly, so called because of its appearance around St Mark's Day on 25 April, and we've come to expect them as the weather starts to warm. Their lifecycle is short and within the next couple of weeks they will disappear as suddenly as they arrived. Swallows dart alongside the hedgerow, making the most of this sudden bonanza while it lasts.

The farm is lush and green. Sunshine yellow dandelions delight pollen-dusted bees as they revel in the nectar buried deep among ragged petals. Bird cherries are in flower and the racemes of blossom shower us with petals like confetti at the slightest breeze. The grass has started to get longer now, and so far we have recorded 38 skylark and 22 meadow pipit territories, all nesting among the tussocky grassland. To avoid any disturbance, I use only the network of tracks that weave across the farm like watermarks, carved out by the footsteps of the animals that traverse it. In sparse patches where damp mud holds onto its memories, it is evident how many species have contributed to forming this web of pathways. The deep parallel grooves of a roe deer's footprint are mimicked by the tiny toes of a delicate muntjac picking its way through the grass. A badger's broad print is characterized by the long, powerful claws that stretch out far beyond the round pads and this is easily distinguished from the agile fox whose pads form a tight diamond. Every so often a meadow pipit materializes from the grass with a sudden flurry of flickering wings. If it is close enough to my path, I can peer into the grass to find a tightly woven nest housing a precious clutch of speckled brown eggs.

The farm is lush and green. Sunshine yellow dandelions delight pollen-dusted bees as they revel in the nectar buried deep among ragged petals.

Towards the top of the field, the vegetation gets a little wilder, and the grass is interwoven with the leaves of plants not yet ready to flower. Curly ragwort leaves with beautiful scalloped edges rub shoulders with feathered fronds of cow parsley and yarrow while bolshy dock leaves assert their dominance over willowherb that points its elegant, almond-shaped leaves towards the sky. White dead-nettles, gentler than their waspy namesake, cluster together in a broad sweep. Their delicately perfumed flowers nestle like pearls under a rosette of leaves, their edges jagged as though trimmed by pinking shears. Brushing past, the tiniest movement draws my eyes to a small patch of mottled brown. There among the nettles are three leverets sitting perfectly still, wide amber eyes taking in my intrusion, but eliciting no response. Unlike their rabbit cousins, who favour the safety of underground burrows, hares give birth above ground, fully clothed and precocious. The mother will leave her young nestled into scrapes, only returning briefly every few hours to feed them. As with all evolved behaviours, this apparent lack of maternal nurturing has a purpose and helps the hares to avoid attracting the attention of predators. The shades of brown in their fur span the spectrum from yellow ochre to burnt sienna and

provide a near-perfect camouflage among early spring grass still muddled by last year's hay. The young will be independent after only three weeks and these leverets look as though they are almost ready to be self-sufficient. After the briefest of exchanged glances, I swiftly move on, my heart pounding and full of nature-fuelled joy.

* * * * *

There is a magical moment in early May when the stars align and in perfect coordination the vegetation surges skywards. An urgency has taken hold, and branches that were bare mere weeks before have come alive in lush green. The verges now stand almost knee-high and clouds of white cow parsley float lazily over the long grasses. In The Park, the grass is sprinkled with lacy white pignut flowers and buttercups that gleam like drops of gold as they reflect the sunlight. Ragged robin is also in flower, its spindly stems topped with tattered pink flowers. It's heartening to witness the return of these plants that belong in wildflower meadows.

The ponds are also coming to life in the most spectacular way. As the years go by, we spend more time getting to know our land and understanding how the changing seasons mould and shape it. We increasingly capture glimpses of its wet past and how different it would have been centuries ago.

The hydrology of land in our country has been changed beyond all recognition over the past few centuries. In order to make it suitable for farming, land drains hide beneath the surface of the soil like a network of arteries and water is directed into straight ditches with the intention of removing it from the land as quickly as possible. Rivers have been canalized to make transport along them more efficient. Dams and weirs obstruct the migratory routes of fish and eels. Chemicals and waste, washed or deliberately pumped into them have poisoned the water, leaving waterways devoid of life. We have lost our understanding of what a river should be. We are so used to imagining a river as a torrent of water rushing though a channel with defined banks that we have forgotten that a river should meander through the land, rolling and falling with the natural topography, its edges shifting and changing, the boundary between land and water capricious and inconstant. Temporary and permanent pools, streams and rivulets should be part of its anatomy and it should fatten and swell with the seasons, spilling out onto a flood plain, nourishing the land that absorbs and holds the water. We have destroyed 90 per cent of our freshwater wetlands in the UK in the last 100 years and with them have gone the species that rely on this important habitat. As climate change brings more extreme weather to our shores, we are beginning to see the impact of our actions. The system we have designed can't cope with the volume of flood water gushing at speed down canalized channels and the results have been burst banks and catastrophic flooding, with many people, homes and businesses devastatingly affected.

Our farm is no different and part of our vision is to try and restore a more natural hydrology to the land. Excavating some shallow wader ponds seemed like a good first step in offering the land a taste of its heritage and seeing how it responded, so two years ago we embarked upon what turned out to be a sizeable project, excavating four ponds covering a total area of around 2 hectares (5 acres). We pulled back the topsoil to reveal a sandy layer above dense blue Kimmeridge clay and a seam of white limestone pebbles sandwiched in between. The majority of life in a pond exists within the first 30 centimetres (12 inches) of water, so we designed our ponds to maximize this shallow 'edge'. We created long, meandering banks, with the deepest parts at the centre around 2 metres (6 foot) deep. As the water levels fluctuate, this also has the advantage of revealing large expanses of mud flat when the water retreats. This is perfect for wading birds that make a living rootling around in wet mud for tasty invertebrates. With the soil that was excavated, we built islands, raised areas and sandy banks that have become a haven for mining bees and other insects.

It has been incredible how quickly nature has moved in and begun to proliferate. Although the ponds are not connected to a watercourse, filling up only with water coming up from the ground and down from the sky, within a year, diving beetles, sticklebacks, pond snails and even leeches had started to appear. Tiny eggs that are perfectly adapted to colonize new water bodies must have arrived clinging to the feet of waterbirds. This proliferation has brought with it a greater abundance of birdlife. Oystercatchers nesting close by come to look for worms in the wet soil. Our nesting lapwings are regular visitors. Grey herons and a snow-white little egret wade elegantly through the shallows picking out prey with a swift stab of their knife-like beaks. Green sandpipers and whooper swans have also dropped in and I can't wait to see who else visits as the ponds mature.

Today, great clouds of black tadpoles are massed together in the shallows and streams of them swim together all in the same direction along an unseen tadpole highway. Poking around in the mud, I come across the discarded exoskeleton of a great diving beetle larva and it's not hard to see what a fearsome predator it must be – 5 centimetres (2 inches) long, it is crowned with long curved pincers that act like hypodermic needles to inject digestive enzymes into its prey before it sucks out the resulting soup. Tadpoles are a favourite snack of these larvae and it's incredible to see the building blocks of these complex webs of ecological interdependence being laid down.

The warm, sunny air surrounding the pond is filled with insects. I spot a mayfly in the grass. It looks like a fairy as it rises and falls, practising its beautiful mating dance. Delicate and intricate, with wings like a stained glass window and a long, striped abdomen that ends in three long streamers, this insect will have spent up to three years as a larva, living among the silt in the bed of a pond or stream. Resembling a Chinese dragon with rows of pulsating, feathery gills and a large head armed with tusks and horns, when it is ready for its first costume change, the nymph's skin takes on a silvery glow as though liquid mercury is coursing through its body. In fact, it is air bubbles that form as the creature metamorphoses, and this air gradually makes it more buoyant. When it hits the surface, a rupture begins to form, and a winged insect emerges from the nymph's discarded clothing. Unique among insects, the mayfly undergoes a second moult to reveal the dancing beauty we are more familiar with. This final incarnation has only one purpose. With no mouthparts or digestive organs, its time in the May sunshine is fleeting and once it has mated, the mass emergence of mayflies provides a feeding bonanza for an abundance of other species.

With an exuberant fanfare, the hawthorn has erupted like a fairy wedding in the hedgerows.

A banded demoiselle damselfly glistens, its slender, iridescent body catching the light as it weaves among the grasses. A four-spotted chaser manoeuvres with incredible dexterity on translucent wings like a tiny helicopter. She lays her eggs on leaves that float just beneath the surface, curving her long body around to deposit them quickly before whizzing off without a second thought. I get a closer look at a recently emerged black-tailed skimmer basking on a blade of grass. The dragonfly is at its most vulnerable after freeing itself from its juvenile exoskeleton. Its body is soft and unprotected, and it needs to inflate its wings, pumping insect 'blood' known as haemolymph through its veins as they unfurl. The new armour plating then begins to harden, equipping it with a rigid protective coating. The whole process takes up to three hours. The dragonfly is alien-like in appearance, with huge, domed eyes that occupy most of its head, and yellow plates covering its body. It gently beats its gossamer wings, testing them out for the first time, before taking off vertically and vanishing into the long spring grasses.

* * * * *

With an exuberant fanfare, the hawthorn has erupted like a fairy wedding in the hedgerows. Young branches laden with thousands of white flowers escape in all directions like Medusa's serpents. The sweet scent wafting away from the hedgerows is powerful and complex, tinged with something primal that seems at odds with the delicate innocence of the white and blush-pink blooms. A component of the hawthorn's scent is trimethylamine. This is the same compound produced by rotting flesh and the plant has evolved to use it to entice the insects that it needs to pollinate its flowers. Living life within the confines of our five senses, it is hard to imagine how other animals may perceive the world and we tend to project upon them our own experience. Under ultraviolet light, we begin to understand that the world exists in a myriad of other dimensions when seen through the filter of another species' senses. A flower suddenly takes on a whole new appearance, with patterns and markings that direct the insect to its heart where the nectar and pollen are found. Bees build up a positive charge on their bodies during flight so negatively charged pollen clings to them when they land on a flower. There is even evidence that bees can 'see' the strength of the electric charge on a flower, guiding them to the ones

with the most pollen. The blooming hawthorn resonates with us deeply, appealing to so many of our senses that it is easy to believe that it exists for our benefit alone and that other animals experience it in the same way that we do, but this is clearly not the case.

In Benard's Field, the lapwings are still busily feeding their chicks. Although they lay their eggs in relatively open ground where they have a good chance of spotting approaching predators, once the chicks hatch they lead them to wetter areas to feed, and the remaining boggy areas of the farm where water still stands is perfect for sustaining them. I stand and watch them for a while when my attention is drawn to a sound I don't recognize. A three-note call, repeated over and over, it sounds like a sort of popping or the peculiar noise made by a wobble board. It is a quail. Often heard but more rarely seen, they prefer to escape danger by running through vegetation rather than revealing their location by flying away. They also have an uncanny ability to throw their voice which helps them to evade predation. These little birds migrate thousands of kilometres from Africa to breed here in the UK. I don't catch a glimpse of the quail, but just hearing one is another first for me. Making new discoveries like this fills both Jack and me with enormous pleasure. We are learning more and more every day about the different species using our land, and it is fuelling the passion that we have for the project, and the fiery determination to continue along this path. It is moments like these that give us the reassurance we sometimes need that we are doing the right thing for our farm.

I scan my binoculars across the landscape and they rest upon another parent taking a breather from the arduous task of feeding hungry young. We have a family of tawny owls in a nest box that we installed in the hedgerow that runs between Lone Pasture and Benard's Field. As the chicks grow and the air warms, we are increasingly seeing the parents sitting on the ledge outside the

box or roosting on top of it. The larger female is now perching on a branch in a field maple further down the hedgerow. The shading of her plumage perfectly mimics the shadows of leaves that float across the trunk of the tree and she blends into the landscape like a chameleon. I manage to capture a few quick sketches and am struck by the perfect symmetry of her face, each half resembling a segment of sliced apple. Her feathery toes terminate in curved claws, needle sharp, and the tattered bark beneath them reveals that this is not the first time she has rested here. Without warning, she drops from her perch, gliding effortlessly on broad wings along the hedgerow before looping over the top and disappearing from sight.

June

I am constantly surprised and delighted by the speed and enthusiasm with which nature has recolonized our farm. The increase in diversity and abundance of plants, insects, birds, amphibians and mammals has been reassuringly rapid and has needed very little intervention from us. I find this a very hopeful message. If we can learn to see beauty in a wilder environment, cease our relentless obsession with tidiness and reduce our reliance on chemicals, even by a small amount, we can expect to see material results very quickly, even if true complexity and stability take longer to achieve. We have so much to gain from making a little more space for nature and it seems that she can be forgiving if we act before it is too late. However, as delighted as we are to see the beginnings of a recovery happening on our very local scale, there are still signs that all is not well.

This is the first year that swallows have not returned to our farm buildings to nest and breed. Last year, two pairs forged their cup-shaped nests from mud and grass nestled into the beams of our vaulted garage roof and inside our barn. We became accustomed to seeing the adults cutting through the air over our heads as they ferried nesting materials, and then insects, into our buildings. We marvelled at them skimming lightly over the surface of the ponds as they hunted and we watched from our bedroom window as fluffy fledglings took their first tentative flights. They were so familiar that we took them for granted. I expected to greet them again this year and to feel the comfort of their presence. This year the barns are empty and it fills me with a sense of lonely foreboding and deep sadness. The broken remains of nests from previous years still cling to the roof and provide a depressing reminder of this year's absence. It is difficult to say why they have not returned, but we know that swallow numbers have been declining since the 1970s. It is thought that climate change is having a serious impact on their migration routes with hotter, drier summers making it harder for them to breed successfully. As pools dry up and insect numbers suffer as a result, the chicks die from heat exhaustion or starvation. The expansion of the Sahara Desert is making it increasingly difficult to cross, and this year Spain was ravaged with extreme heat waves and droughts, which could have impacted migrations.

We also experienced a summer last year that felt apocalyptic in its conditions. Severe drought was compounded by temperatures that reached 40 degrees Celsius and the countryside was parched and brown by August. This year, the signs all indicate that this has had a devastating effect on insect populations across the country. #silentspring is trending on social media, and hundreds of people are reporting blooming hedgerows devoid of hoverflies and bees, meadows bright with flowers that have no pollinators and blue tits abandoning their broods because they can find nothing to feed them with. Butterflies seem to have suffered in particular – with no food for their caterpillars as plants withered and scorched in the summer heat, numbers have fallen dramatically. Meadow brown, a grassland species, is one that is likely to have been affected. Last year, as the thistles bloomed in Fox Cover in late spring, thousands of meadow brown butterflies lifted from the flowers in a huge billowing cloud. It was the very definition of breathtaking abundance and a long-forgotten spectacle that should be commonplace on our islands. Although it is usual to see annual fluctuations in insect numbers, this year feels different, and I am nervous about the cascading effects of these crumbling foundations.

In brighter news, the lone marsh orchid that had appeared in the margins of Benard's Field last year has multiplied, and there is now a cluster of six shyly emerging from the tangle of grasses at the edge of the wood. With their extravagant beauty, these flowers symbolize the ephemeral fragility of nature, and their return to the farm feels important. Part of the reason for this fragility exists beneath the surface of the soil. Orchids have a unique and intimate relationship with mycorrhizal fungi. Their tiny seeds lack energy reserves, and they forge a parasitic relationship with fungi, extracting the nutrients they need in order to germinate. As the orchid grows, the relationship with the fungus becomes mutually beneficial, and in return for providing the orchid with nutrients the fungus receives sugars and other organic compounds. The dousing of soil with fungicides and the destruction of its structure with cultivation disrupts this delicate relationship and is partially why orchids are vanishingly rare in our countryside.

We also have some new arrivals to the pond – a pair of little grebes arrived a few weeks ago and have begun to build a nest. Breaking through the surface of the water, a jumble of pondweed and grasses woven together and anchored to reeds, their nest

is steadily growing day by day. Fascinating to watch, the grebes are continually bobbing under the water diving for prey – insect larvae, molluscs and even small fish – before a little head emerges halfway across the pond. In two short years, it is incredible that the ponds now have enough life within them to support an ever-increasing abundance of species. Gazing across the surface that glistens and dances with skaters and mosquitos, untroubled by the gaping beak of a predatory swallow, I am reminded that we can't exist in isolation and bigger change is needed to restore the natural order to our wild isles.

* * * * *

The tawny owl fledglings are now starting to make an appearance, perching on the ledge that sits around the owl box. They still lack the sleek, dappled plumage of the adults and appear downy and grey, a pale barred pattern just visible like ripples on sand. They haven't yet grown into their beaks, which protrude, disproportionately large, from their fluffy faces, giving them a slightly awkward appearance. They test their wings, stretching them out as they try to get the measure of these ungainly appendages. We also spotted another pair of fledgling tawny owls sunning themselves in a hawthorn tree just on the other side of Fox Cover, around 1 kilometre (⅔ mile) away from the box. Tawny owls are fiercely territorial creatures and it's a good sign that the habitat is rich enough with voles to support two broods in such close proximity.

The tree sparrows and blue tits that nest under the pan tiles of our roof have also fledged. I peeked into one of the cocoon-like cavities and found nests lined with a distinctive mixture of ginger and black curls – remnants from the last haircut of our toy poodles, Claude and Elvis. A pair of pied wagtails has opportunistically built a nest, now full of gaping beaks, just behind the bonnet of a tractor that was parked outside the shed between jobs and is now rendered out of action for a while. In an old rose that rambles over an archway in the garden, a pair of industrious mistle thrushes, having already fledged one brood, is rearing a second. Tall, sandy-coloured birds, freckled with dark arrowheads on their breasts, we've been watching them for weeks now tirelessly ferrying food to their young. As they grow, the chicks are almost spilling out of the messy nest that the thrushes seem to have thrown together haphazardly. Ferociously territorial, their loud, grating alarm call sounds like a claxon every time we open the back door.

The lapwing juveniles have moved over to the pond with the adults now and they hide among the long grasses at the margins. A pair of oystercatchers seems to favour a sandy island in one of the ponds, probing their long red beaks into the soft, damp edges, every so often letting off a volley of piping calls. The tadpoles are still grouped together in a great black mass, but a closer look reveals little legs, and the most advanced are already starting to venture out of the water. The muddy edge of the pond is wriggling with tiny wet toadlets, as small as my little fingernail. They crawl and hop along the sand, the smallest bump posing an obstacle of gigantic proportions. The waterlilies floating on the pond have sent up fat buds and the air is full of dragonflies and damselflies. Little black beetles chase one another over the surface like bumper cars, and endlessly moving clouds of flies hover above it, each cluster a single dynamic organism. The little grebes are now incubating eggs on their floating nest. Built for diving, they clamber out of the water onto their island of pond weed with laborious effort, their little legs seeming insufficient to hold their dumpy, round bodies aloft.

> The carnival of hawthorn has ended and now the delicate and understated pink blossoms of dog rose and brambles decorate the hedgerows.

It is a warm evening and I'm enjoying being outside after a long day. The spring is maturing into summer and the grasses are in flower, painting a purple haze over the fields with their feathery ears. It glistens in the evening sunlight and moves like a rippling ocean in the light breeze. Grasses including meadow foxtail and Yorkshire fog quiver among clovers, trefoils and knapweeds, while cadmium red poppies are dotted like jewels under a canopy of lacy hogweed umbels. The carnival of hawthorn has ended and now the delicate and understated pink blossoms of dog rose and brambles decorate the hedgerows.

A pair of roe deer are grazing in Fox Cover, their heads just visible above the long grass. Immediately alerted by my presence, we all stand perfectly still observing one another. The male raises his moustachioed face, his sensitive nostrils detecting my scent

on the air. The rut hasn't yet started but soon testosterone will start to flood through his veins, he will become aggressive and territorial, and the eternal battle to pass on his genes will begin in earnest. Roe deer have delayed implantation and although mating will occur over the summer, the embryo won't start to develop until around January, and the dappled fawns will be born in May or June next year. Scanning over the long grasses, I am sure there will be one of this year's newborn roe fawns nestled among them, safely cocooned and camouflaged by the ripening vegetation.

A rustling in the grass beside me takes my gaze away from the deer. A young badger is snuffling away in the grass and stops in his tracks when he spots me. With surprising agility that defies his rotund appearance, he careers off into the long grass in the direction of the sett, and I get a good view of his round, silvery bottom before he disappears from sight. Looking back in the direction of the deer, I am just in time to see another two bottoms, this time snowy white as they bound away like gymnasts.

* * * * *

We have several badger setts on the farm. The largest is on the edge of The Park and the residents leave plenty of evidence of their presence. This ranges from footprints by the pond, their long digging claws leaving imprints in the soft mud, to the latrines that are dotted around the sett and nose-sized, crescent-shaped divots excavated in the short grass where they have snuffled about for worms. However, they are elusive creatures, and we are rarely treated to more than the most fleeting of glimpses at dusk. We get our best sightings on the trail cameras that we place strategically around the farm, and we've begun to recognize some of the individuals with distinctive features, which help to distinguish them from their sett-mates.

Given the rarity of these encounters, I was surprised to see the same young badger that I had disturbed previously, a few nights later on the shallow bank of the pond. He didn't stick around for very long before shuffling off into the long grass, but even more surprisingly, he is there again this evening. I have Claude and Elvis with me and all of us are so surprised to see the badger just a couple of metres in front of us that we freeze. I'm pretty sure that if they ended up in a scuffle our toy poodles wouldn't come out on top, so I call to them and they stop straining on their long leads and trot back to me, all the while keeping a suspicious eye firmly fixed on the strange intruder. With all of this disturbance I expect the badger to make a sharp exit, but after weighing us up he just carries on with his business, snuffling at the edge of the pond. Suddenly the penny drops. He is in exactly the same location as the toadlets that have started to emerge from the ponds. Evidently the culinary jackpot he has stumbled across is worth tolerating our presence for and he laps them up from the damp soil with a sticky pink tongue. As adults, toads secrete a toxin from their skin that makes them unpalatable and offers them some protection against predation. The tadpoles also contain a toxin and this gives them a survival advantage over the more appetizing frog tadpoles in ponds with fish. However, this doesn't seem to be deterring the badger, as he continues to hoover up the tiny toadlets.

The survival odds for common toads are pretty slim. The population in the UK declined by 68 per cent in the 30 years to 2016*. This is partly because of the wholesale loss of pond habitat across the country. In the past, muddy ponds in corners of fields would have been used as water sources for cattle but we now pipe water to drinking troughs, and the landscape has been tidied and drained, so this vital habitat has all but disappeared.

*According to research undertaken by the charity Froglife, 2016.

Many of the ponds that remain are polluted with pesticides and agricultural run-off, and the absorbent skin of toads seems to make them particularly susceptible to the chemicals that poison their environment. The network of roads that covers the whole country like a fine mesh has also had a massive impact on common toads. As they migrate from damp woodlands and hedgerows where they overwinter to their breeding ponds and summer feeding sites, they are forced to cross some of the 421,500 kilometres (262,000 miles) of road that snake across the countryside. Even without these man-made hazards, pressures from predators and competition for food mean that toad reproduction is all about playing the odds. A single female can produce between 4,000 and 8,000 eggs in a single season, strung together in gelatinous ribbons. Only a very small percentage of these eggs will survive to adulthood. The little toads in our pond are just embarking on the treacherous migration out of the pond to the woodland and hedgerows where they will spend the autumn and winter before returning to their natal ponds again in spring for breeding. Even this exodus is timed to help increase their chances of survival – the toadlets all become mature enough to leave the pond within a couple of days of one another, and they will leave *en masse*, overwhelming any predators and giving them the best chances of survival. Despite knowing this, I feel very invested in these toads. Every day since February I've been heading to the pond, anxiously looking out for the spawn and reporting back to my long-suffering family. When the toads eventually arrived, I've watched the little blobs of jelly change and develop as the little black nuclei developed tails and eventually morphed into toads, each one a miracle. Observing nature is an emotional rollercoaster, and it's impossible not to be affected by the life and death battles that are continually being played out, particularly at this time of year when the stakes are high and species of almost every denomination are competing and jostling to pass their genes on to the next generation. Watching the exertions of adult birds as they build nests and tirelessly feed their young only to have them predated by jays and magpies is particularly painful. However, predation is normal, and in a balanced system, should not affect the overall survival of a prey species. It is only in degraded and incomplete environments that predation becomes a problem and threatens to overwhelm entire species. As a result, we often unfairly demonize predators, casting them as the enemy rather than reflecting upon our own role in the breakdown of these delicate relationships. It is so important not to let our human emotions get the better of us, but to see predators as a vital part of a functioning, healthy ecosystem.

So, Claude, Elvis and I quietly back away and let the toad vs badger battle play out as nature intended. We walk back through The Park, enjoying the sunshine as dragonflies and damselflies burst out of the grass like sea spray with every footstep. A pair of grey partridges makes us jump as we disturb them, indignantly calling out in shrill voices as their little wings whirr furiously with the effort of keeping their round bodies aloft.

* * * * *

One of the most exciting developments on the farm, which is happening with astonishing speed, is the process of natural regeneration. Decades of intensive cultivation and drenching the land with fertilizers and pesticides has destroyed vital bacteria and fungi in the soil and disrupted its complex structure. Modern, industrialized farming techniques are accelerating a worrying trend across the globe. Soils, vital for sustaining life as we know it, are undergoing erosion, compaction, nutrient imbalance, pollution, acidification and loss of biodiversity. This, in turn, reduces the soil's ability to support plant life and grow crops. It has been widely quoted that UK arable soils can support only another 100 harvests if action is not taken to restore and repair our land.

By taking machinery and chemicals off the land we are giving our soil an opportunity to heal. With no pesticides, the biodiversity of the soil can begin to improve. Microbes, fungi, earthworms and other soil-dwelling organisms aid nutrient cycling and deposition of organic matter, which will start to rebuild the soil structure. In addition, we are starting to see the establishment of a rich and diverse community of plants colonizing the soil. These early pioneers will be succeeded by different plants as the land matures, and already we see flushes of plants appearing and disappearing every year, and areas of the farm look wildly different from one another despite having had broadly the same treatment. At the moment, Fox Cover looks particularly beautiful. Feathery purple grasses intermingle with stately stands of viper's-bugloss that emerge poker straight beside swathes of clover and bird's-foot trefoil. Spear thistles are just beginning to flower while delicate vetch weaves its tendrils around the stems. The penetration of all of these root systems, each with different strategies for finding water and nutrients, will enhance soil aeration, water movement and nutrient distribution. Their probing fingers will break up the compaction and begin to bring life back to the soils. As they die back, their decaying bodies will add organic matter, cycling back into the soil through the actions of earthworms and other soil dwelling organisms.

At the south end of Benard's Field, the vegetation looks altogether different. The copses that overshadow it have begun to bleed out into the field itself. Silver birches with quivering leaves and sallow saplings stand 2.5 metres (8 foot) tall among dog rose, hawthorn and blackthorn, where just a few years ago a barren tilth stood empty. Sallow is a particularly important pioneer species. It has deep and vigorous roots that kick start the process of structural repair and it is also able to absorb heavy metals from the soil, helping to reverse the impact of soil pollution. In addition, it provides a vital food source and habitat for an abundance of different species.

Across the farm, saplings of another important species are springing up like little beacons of hope and optimism. Oak is clearly a species that is well suited to our land. Throughout the course of a season, jays bury thousands of acorns, caching them away for future consumption. They have remarkable memories and retrieve many acorns that sustain them throughout leaner months. However, some of the acorns will remain buried and forgotten about, dispersed effectively from the parent tree and will germinate and grow. On pretty much any of our land that has been left untouched, you will find oak trees in varying stages of maturity. Some succumb to the nibbling mouths of browsing deer, but some, particularly those sheltered among a shroud of thorny scrub, escape

and are able to thrive. This year's crop is just visible among short vegetation: perfectly formed lobed leaves attached to woody little stems. In the margins of Fox Cover where they have had a head start over the past decade, bushy plants stand above head height, the ridged stems already taking on the character of a mature oak. In a patch of tall blackthorn at the corner of Fox Cover, the top of an oak tree has started to emerge, with 60cm (2 foot) of leafy branches now visible above the crown of the spiny thicket. Scrub like this is described as the 'nursery of the oak', its spines and dense cover protecting the tender oak shoots from hungry mouths and trampling feet. When scrub and oaks are allowed to grow together like this there is no need for plastic tree guards.

Mature trees are in short supply on our 120 hectares (300 acres). We have just a small handful that escaped the axe as the land was cleared to make way for bigger machinery and more efficient practices, and among them are a few oaks, centuries old. These trees are not pinned into woodland and forced to grow poker straight to reach the light in competition with their neighbours. Instead, their branches twist and turn, spreading and sprawling away from the gnarled trunk and resting on the ground in places in a deep curtsy. Gaping holes where branches have been lost in long-forgotten storms provide nesting sites for cavity-nesting birds, owls, squirrels and bats. The bark is deeply textured like ancient skin. Its grooves and crevices provide habitat for insects and beetles that in turn attract the birds and mammals that feed on them. Mosses, liverworts and lichens cling to branches like jewels, and fungi thrive in the damp micro-environments created by the folds and ridges in the crenelated bark. The canopy is inhabited by another suite of organisms that feed on the leaves and the purple hairstreak butterfly is one that we've spotted among the leaves of our oaks. Gall wasps lay their eggs in developing leaf buds and this stimulates biochemical changes in the tree itself, disrupting the

normal growth pattern of the bud and forming a gall. The tree has essentially created a safe nursery in which the wasp larvae can feed and remain protected until they are ready to disperse. The galls do no harm to the tree and even the youngest oak saplings on the farm are decorated with little brown galls, the tiny holes evidence of where the wasps escaped from their protective cocoon.

One of Jack's favourite sayings is that the best time to plant a tree was 20 years ago, but the second-best time is now. We will never see the saplings that have rooted here become gnarled giants. Even our children won't see them reach their full potential, and I wonder who will be gazing upon these oak trees in centuries to come. I hope that they will be able to enjoy a rich and diverse landscape, abundant and wild, and I hope that they will love it as much as we do.

* * * * *

It's late June, but following recent patterns, it is unseasonably warm and hot air sits heavily over the farm. Other than a few days of light rain that barely slaked the thirst of the greedy soil, it has been exceptionally dry of late. The land that wanted to be wet all winter dried out quickly once the rain stopped, in part thanks to the network of land drains that sit unseen under the surface, laid down by farmers of the past. The clay soil is hard and dusty. Wide fissures have opened up like old wounds. Plants with shallow root systems have already started to lose turgidity in the drought, their heads drooping under the weight of fat buds on flaccid stems.

Butterflies have finally started to emerge in larger numbers now and although some species are notably absent or thin on the ground after the excruciating heat last summer, it's heartening to see that we still have some degree of abundance, and meadow browns, skippers, small heaths and ringlets dance among the flowers. Their fluttery, uneven flight is light and delicate as they navigate the long grass, in total contrast with the precision manoeuvres of the hunting dragonflies with whom they share the habitat. This is the second year that we have been professionally monitoring numbers of Odonata (dragonflies and damselflies) and Lepidoptera (butterflies and moths) on the farm, and seeing how quickly the numbers have responded to the easing of man-made pressures on the land has been one of the most satisfying successes so far. On seeing this year's survey we were told by a local lepidopterist that our farm is likely to be one of the best sites in Lincolnshire for grassland species. In a few short years, our land, which was one of the worst sites for arable farming in the county, has transformed into one of the best for grassland butterflies. It is an incredible metamorphosis and helps to reinforce my conviction that we have made the right decision. Rather than forcing the land to grow crops that it struggled to nurture even with our heavy-handed interventions, we have trusted it to shape its own destiny and it is excelling.

Despite the dry spell, the ponds are still remarkably full thanks to the blue clay that we sit on. The shallow banks mean that the smallest drop in water levels reveals an expanse of wet mud wriggling with invertebrates and whole bank is decorated with the criss-crossing footprints of the birds that feed there. As well as the invertebrate life that has populated the ponds, plants have begun to colonize as well, and water mint, common reeds and water-loving rushes have all started to appear. New ponds are an important habitat type in themselves and many species specialize in colonizing them. By attempting to intervene and planting and populating them ourselves we rob many invertebrates and plants an opportunity to thrive. In fact, new ponds are rich in biodiversity, sometimes even more so than older, established ponds.

One small intervention that we decided to make more recently was to drag some branches from the coppice into the margin of the ponds. Fallen branches and decaying wood are natural features of aquatic environments. They create miniature ecosystems offering food and protection to invertebrates and other aquatic organisms.

I take a walk to the ponds this evening and through the binoculars scan quickly across the margins. My eyeline drifts over the tangle of twigs and branches that emerges from the glassy surface of the pond and suddenly catches upon a flash of iridescent blue. A beautiful male kingfisher is perched upon a branch and is using it as a vantage point from which to hunt. It's so rare to get a good look at these beautiful birds; we've seen them before in the tightly woven hedges that line the becks and dykes around the farm, but we are usually treated to a cursory flash of blue and orange before they disappear like an arrow. He is small, not much bigger than a robin, but the metallic shimmer of his feathers is startling. The cyan feathers in fact contain no blue pigment, the colour we see is the result of the complex structure within the feather and the way it reflects the light that shines on it. The orange of the underbelly would appear almost exactly opposite the blue on a colour wheel – the contrast is shockingly stark and jarring, each colour accentuating the other to the best possible effect as they sit strikingly next to one another. The gun-metal grey beak is sharp and strong. Females have a flush of orange on the lower part of the beak and the solid grey is how I can identify this bird as a male. Without warning, his sharp eyes spot what he has been looking for and he fires into the pond, cutting through the surface in a frictionless slice, emerging again in a perfect arc with a tiny fish.

July

Having made several fruitless evening excursions down to the village end of Benard's Field in search of the grasshopper warbler, I am surprised to hear a distinctive trilling sound ringing through the air at the bottom of our driveway as I head to collect the post. It can be difficult to pinpoint the source of a grasshopper warbler's song. They move their heads from side to side as they sing, flinging their voice in all directions, allowing the notes to reverberate and reflect, confusing any potential predator as to their location. Any thoughts of collecting the post are abandoned and I head into the Vicar's Field, the most likely source of the sound. A few years ahead of the rest of the farm in terms of the development of thorny scrub, the Vicar's Field is rich habitat. Adolescent hawthorn and dog rose rub shoulders with sallow, bramble and blackthorn among swaying grasses, wild flowers and even a random patch of water mint that thrives in a damp area of the field. Butterflies do well here, and we have seen common lizards basking on dusty bare soil outside a long-abandoned barn, which is littered with owl pellets. Sure enough, perched upon a thorny arc of dog rose, a grasshopper warbler is in full song. His wide gape is framed by the sharply pointed beak of an insectivore and his slim body shape identifies him as part of the warbler family. The Vicar's Field is about 1.6km (1 mile) away from the newly planted wood at the top of Benard's Field so it's not clear if this is the same bird that had been heard earlier in the season or if this is a different male in search of a mate. A summer migrant from Africa, this little brown bird is unassuming, his sandy plumage making him very difficult to tell apart visually from other warblers that arrive in the UK to breed. But his call is unique and needs no explanation beyond his perfectly apt name. As he sings from his perch, he attracts the interest of some recently fledged whitethroats who are clearly intrigued and confused by his soprano vibrations, indicating that he may be a new arrival to this little patch of habitat. I linger for a while, savouring the evening sunshine, but the horse flies are also doing well along the ditches that surround the field and having endured a few sharp bites I decide to head back home.

At the side of the mown path, a patch of brown fur catches my eye and I poke around in the long grass to investigate further. A large rat, having met some kind of untimely end, lies among the thatch. Belly-up, its pink claws are balled into rigor-induced fists and its mouth is slightly agape revealing long, yellow teeth. Investigating the corpse like prospective buyers viewing a new build are a pair of orange and black striped beetles. Burying beetles have receptors on their antennae that allow them to detect the scent of rotting flesh from up to 1.6 kilometres (1 mile) away. Arriving upon a fresh corpse, a male and female will pair up and set to work burying their quarry, ferociously defending it against other beetles that are also attracted by the smell of death. Once it is buried, the female lays her eggs and, unusual among insects, both male and female beetles nurture their young, feeding them on the rotting body of their host.

Life and death are close companions in nature and the margin that exists between the two can be achingly narrow. Fierce battles for survival rage on every front and this drives the powerful force of natural selection that is responsible for the huge variety of life on Earth. The burying beetles and their macabre way of life are a reminder that life exists in death and that nature has provided a full suite of organisms that complete the circle, recycling nutrients and ensuring that nothing is wasted. It is yet another aspect of the natural world that we have disrupted and destroyed. Our endless obsession with sanitizing nature and efficiently tidying away, even down to removing fallen trees, deprives a whole host of species that specialize in processing death of their livelihood. The cycles that existed for millennia before we graced the planet with our presence are disturbed and broken. Eventually, I head back to collect my post. A bill and a couple of pieces of junk mail. It is suddenly unimportant beside the adventures of grasshopper warblers, dead bodies and burying beetles.

* * * * *

Meadowsweet has erupted into effervescent flower alongside the dykes. Frothy exuberances the colour of cloudy lemonade are held aloft on dark red stems. Its marzipan fragrance drifts over from the hedgerow. At the ponds, huge emperor dragonflies have emerged, glinting turquoise and emerald in the sunlight, and they patrol their territories alongside banded demoiselles and broad-bodied chasers. The little grebes are having a second attempt at incubating a clutch of eggs. Their first nest, inadequately anchored to a patch of reeds,

blew to the side of the
pond during a storm,
where the eggs must have
made easy pickings
for passing predators.
High above the pond,
sooty-coloured swifts
with white beards appear
like dark crescents
against the summer
sky as they circle in
wide arcs. Swifts spend
most of their lives on
the wing, eating, mating,
bathing and even sleeping in flight.
Their similarities to swallows and martins are superficial. It is
an example of convergent evolution – the development of similar
advantageous characteristics in unrelated animals due to them
occupying a similar niche with similar evolutionary pressures.
Swifts are more closely related to hummingbirds than they are to
swallows. Climate change and the precipitous collapse of insect
numbers over the last few decades is having a devastating impact
on these birds that are steadily disappearing from our skies. The
'screaming parties', gatherings of large numbers of swifts on long,
warm evenings calling to one another in their distinctive high-
pitched squeals, are in danger of becoming a thing of historic
summers, existing only in the memories of those lucky enough to
have heard them in a more abundant past. As our homes become
more impermeable and energy efficient, the holes and cavities that
swifts rely on as nesting sites are also disappearing. This year, I
put up swift nesting boxes around our eaves, but so far they have
remained empty.

The wild cherries are now bearing small, tart fruits that shine like polished gems. Blackbirds sit among the ridged leaves and gorge on the ruby treasures that hang from branches in clusters. It's clear that other animals are also enjoying the early fruiting of the wild cherry trees. Piles of hedgehog and fox scat deposited all around the farm are stained crimson red and studded with seeds. Alongside the birds, these mammals are playing an important role in dispersing the cherry's potential offspring, and it is likely that some of these seeds will find the right conditions to germinate. We have some wild cherry trees in the garden and I have a perfect view of them from my bedroom window where I sit and drink my first coffee of the day. I pull back the curtain and fortunately don't draw any attention to myself. Underneath the trees, rootling among the grass for the fallen cherries that cover the ground like marbles, a vixen and two cubs are foraging. It's a rare opportunity to observe and sketch the foxes.

Foxes are ever present on the farm and they are among my very favourite animals. We catch momentary glimpses of them, especially in the autumn and winter when they are not concealed by the verdant foliage of the warmer months. They are often captured by the trail cameras secreted around the farm and this vixen and her mate have been raising their family in the little copse at the edge of Fox Cover. I've seen her trotting past carrying food into the den including a mole and an enormous hare that must have lingered somewhere for too long. The cubs are inquisitive and playful, and even in the garden with a bonanza of ripe cherries to graze on they are distracted by one another, pouncing and rolling, flexing their muscles in preparation for their independence. It is unusual to see foxes like this so close to human habitation. These are country foxes. They don't have the wily brazenness of their city-dwelling cousins that are even evolving shorter, less aggressive-looking faces in order to be more appealing to the eyes of their human

benefactors. The vixen is wary. Her ears are in constant motion and every few seconds she looks up from the cherries, surveying her surroundings with sharp, amber eyes. Eventually she decides that the risks of remaining any longer outweigh the bounty of cherries and a silent communication passes between the three of them. The cubs cease their play and follow their mother's flame-coloured tail as she leads them back into the safety of the hedgerow.

* * * * *

July is in full flow and the air feels thick and lazy. The grass has given up its colour and shades of gold and ochre glimmer in the haze that settles over the field. The birds are quieter now, exhausted and shabby from the exertions of rearing this year's young, but grasshoppers have started to sing and the fields fizz and hum with their vibrations. It is the perfect month for butterflies, and after a slow start, the farm is filled with their flutterings. Creeping thistle is thick and dense in some areas, a mauve carpet bleeding into the landscape. It thrums with life. Ladybirds feeding on aphids that are farmed by ants patrolling up and down the stems form a community on one plant. Red admiral, meadow brown and peacock butterflies dance around the flowers, using their long proboscises to extract nectar. Furry bees bumble from one flower to the next. Shiny, bulbous tumours on stems house the larvae of gall flies that are feasting on its internal organs. Other insects and beetles of all kinds are making use of this unloved plant, from stem to seed.

July is in full flow and the air feels thick and lazy.
The grass has given up its colour and shades
of gold and ochre glimmer in the haze.

But there is a prevailing wind that blows towards the village and it has already started to pick up diaphanous seeds that float like fairies on the slightest breeze. Creeping thistle is considered a pernicious weed and can spread with astonishing vigour. It was labelled as such in the days before farmers drenched their land with chemicals to prevent weeds competing with their crops, but the law still requires their spread to be controlled. We have left it as long as possible but with a heavy heart we are forced to cut the heads off the thistles in the thickest patches in an attempt to stop the seeds blowing towards the village. Clouds of insects billow ahead of the blade. We leave as much as we dare.

Ragwort too must be dealt with. Its golden flowers are a vital source of food for many insects and more than 30 species feed on it exclusively. Sure enough, many of the plants are infested with stripy orange and black caterpillars, the larvae of the cinnabar moth. Comb-footed spiders with bulbous abdomens striped like humbugs lurk behind petals laying traps for visiting insects. Hoverflies delicately alight on nectar-filled flowers. A closer look at just one plant reveals an abundance of diversity supported by these golden daisies. Our management plan for ragwort is to keep the 50-metre (165-foot) strip alongside our neighbour's property clear as this exceeds the distance over which the seeds are able to spread. This prevents the plant from spreading from our land to any fields nearby that will be cut for hay, where it can be deadly to livestock. Fortunately, this management plan is less destructive than that of the thistles. We painstakingly pull the plants out by hand and lay them in patches of ragwort in the centre of the farm to allow the caterpillars and other insects to find another host.

It's a hard day, and we feel deeply conflicted about having to intervene in this way.

I walk back across the farm towards the ponds. A crouching hare's black-tipped ears are just visible above the sward, tilting and rotating like satellite dishes. As I walk alongside Fox Cover, I spot a bird around the size of a kestrel circling low over the grasses. Its body shape resembles a falcon and it has the tear marks streaking down its face, but its movements are not those of a kestrel and its wings are longer and slimmer, creating a silhouette against the sky almost like that of a swift. The final giveaway is the rusty red trousers out of which bright yellow legs protrude. It is a hobby and I am beside myself with excitement. I've never seen a hobby on the farm. Perfectly designed for agile manoeuvres, it specializes in pursuing the most acrobatic of prey, from dragonflies to swallows and martins. The new ponds have yet again yielded treasure by providing habitat for the hobby's favourite food. It arcs through the sky like a scythe while being mobbed by a group of swallows from above, and with a sudden movement, a fat dragonfly is in its talons.

It passes the insect deftly between its claws and its curved beak and circles round again, ignoring the swallows that are understandably upset by its presence. It turns its attention for a while to some butterflies before disappearing over the hedge.

* * * * *

For my birthday last year, Jack bought me a moth trap. Despite the murderous sounding name, it is a tool ecologists use for monitoring and observing moths, which are then released unharmed. It consists of a box that houses a light tube, and in place of a lid it has two clear Perspex sheets that slope down leaving a narrow opening in the middle allowing the moths that have been attracted by the light to enter, but making it a little more difficult for them to leave. Torn up egg boxes are placed in the box offering nooks and crannies for the moths to hide in. The next morning after a night of moth trapping, it's like opening a box of treasure and seeing what little jewels are hiding inside. Identifying the moths is not an easy task – there are around 2,500 different moth species in the UK and some of them look incredibly similar. I am nothing more than a keen amateur but absolutely love checking my moth trap in the morning armed with my sketch book and a little ID guide. Collecting this data will help us to monitor the impact that the changes on the farm are having over time on these important insects. Even with my limited expertise, I'm starting to recognize the common species – the ermines with snowy white boas draped around their shoulders, the angle shades and setaceous Hebrew characters with cryptic symbols painted on their wings. My favourites are the hawk moths – enormous and eccentrically beautiful. Elephant hawk moths are fuchsia pink and green, named because their caterpillar resembles an elephant's trunk. Eyed hawk moths have scalloped wings with a mottled

Silky beige

Antled of leaf

Poplar Hawk Moth

Perfect camouflage

Thickly feathered antennae

Back wings in front to front wings

Eyed Hawk moth

Tail curled up

Chocolate brown shades

Well camouflaged until it reveals bright blue eyes and flash of pink

Elephant Hawk Moth

Bright Pink hind wings

Comb antennae

Pale Tussock

Very furry body

White Ermine Moth

White furry body

Pink & olive green

Setaceous hebrew character

Alabaster wings

Wings overlap

Twig like appearance

pattern that perfectly camouflages it against the bark of a tree until it suddenly reveals a pair of shocked-looking blue eyes on rose pink hindwings if disturbed.

Today, a beautiful poplar hawk moth has been seduced by the allure of the moth trap's light. Holding its hindwings before its forewings, it has a slightly back-to-front appearance and the intricately patterned dusty wings flank a fat, furry body that curls up behind it and sturdy antennae bearing filaments like little combs. These short-lived moths have no mouth parts for feeding but rely on the fat reserves that were accrued by the caterpillar as it gorged on poplar, willow and sallow – trees that should thrive on our farm as it is allowed to get wetter and wilder.

> Eyed hawk moths have scalloped wings with a mottled pattern that perfectly camouflages it against the bark of a tree until it suddenly reveals a pair of shocked-looking blue eyes on rose pink hindwings if disturbed.

There seems to be little argument about the need to provide nectar-rich flowers for butterflies and moths, and indeed there is no hardship in seeing swathes of brightly coloured flowers in gardens and parks, but it is often the lack of caterpillar food plants that is the limiting factor in Lepidopteran success. Many plants relied upon by caterpillars are unloved and unwanted species: the untidy plants we clear away with impunity. Nettles, dock, thistles, ragwort, willowherb, ivy, bramble and native grasses left to grow long are all important food sources for moth and butterfly caterpillars, and sadly all are seen as pests to be tamed and bullied into submission.

Later that evening, I decide to try out another piece of technology that has been waiting for a still, clear night. Just as the sun begins to descend, I head out down the track towards Basra Wood with a bat detector plugged into my phone. Bats hunt using echolocation. Sending out pulses of sound at a wavelength beyond our hearing range, their powerful ears detect the vibrations returning as they reflect off moths and other insects, enabling them to locate and catch them. Their hearing is so sensitive that a long-eared brown bat has been shown to detect the sound of a ladybird walking on a leaf. A common pipistrelle bat can eat up to 3,500 insects every night – their voracious appetite means that their presence is a good indicator of a healthy insect population. As with all life and death battles, evolution has not left the bat's prey defenceless. Some moths have evolved ears to detect bat echolocation calls, others produce ultrasonic sounds that jam bat signals, and some moths have evolved adaptations for silent flight and wingbeat modulation that makes them harder for the bats to detect.

The piece of kit I have plugged into my phone is able to detect the sound waves emitted by bats. An app then interprets the information and identifies the species. The first species it picks up, just as the sun begins to set, is a noctule. I can't even see this bat let alone hear it, but repeated and strong signals indicate that it is indeed flying somewhere high above the tree line. Noctules are tree dwellers, which take advantage of holes and cavities left by woodpeckers or fallen branches and are usually the first to emerge as the light fades. They are the largest bats in the UK, and they fly high and fast, diving steeply to catch their prey. Then I see my first bat. Flickering against an indigo sky lit by a milky white moon, a leathery little bat flits along the hedgerow. It is a common pipistrelle. Fluttery and darting, its erratic flight pattern makes it adept at catching insects, accelerating and changing direction quickly when hunting. The detector also picks up the other two species of pipistrelle – the Nathusius' and soprano. The

three species of pipistrelle were only recently separated – the main identifying feature being the different frequency of their calls. As night falls and the silhouettes of the trees begin to fade against the darkening sky, the detector is beeping away excitedly, its sensors lit up by the vibrations of the tiny pipistrelles that are flitting around the hedgerow. As I head back inside, I take a detour by the pond and the detector fleetingly picks up the calls of a Daubenton's bat. This is a bat of wetlands and water – it flies low over ponds and watercourses, skimming insects from the surface. I hang around for another little while but with no more sign of the bat.

It's getting cold so I head for home, determining to sit by the ponds for longer next time.

* * * * *

The long, mild evenings of mid-summer feel like stolen time. Hours of daylight snatched from the night and bathed in the tender light of a sinking sun. As each day passes, the night takes back a few more minutes with the certainty of an encroaching tide as the summer ebbs by. It's one of my favourite times to be outside, and after a long day at work, I've come to investigate some animal tracks of flattened vegetation that emerge from the beck bordering Fox Cover. Otters use the becks and dykes like a highway as they travel between their hunting ponds, and we've picked them up before on the trail cameras, so I've decided to place one here to see if it is otters that are coming up out of the beck and forming these tracks through the reeds and grasses. The beck forms the border of our land and is officially recorded as a chalk stream. Pure and clear water that percolates through chalk bedrock and flows along gravelly beds form these special water courses. They are precious and rare habitats that support a huge abundance and diversity of life: 85–90 per cent of chalk streams globally are found in England, and a large number of these flow from the Lincolnshire Wolds. Unfortunately, our murky beck bears little resemblance to these fabled ecosystems. The original meandering stream has long since been diverted and straightened, and the run off of fertilizers, pesticides and topsoil from agricultural fields upstream has reduced it to little more than a silted channel that blooms with algae, duckweed and common reed.

On the other side of the beck, our neighbour has taken a cut of hay from his field and a band of six hares are sparring on the short turf. They lollop and lope as though their unwieldy hind feet are too big for their bodies, occasionally flicking them into the air in a momentary display of power. When gentle teasing turns to irritation, they rear up, arching their long bodies into athletic curves, fists poised to box, but the tension soon melts away in a lazy July scuffle, totally lacking in the high octane, hormone-driven energy of March.

Having put the camera in place, I complete the circuit around the perimeter of Fox Cover and round onto the track back to the house. I catch my breath and check myself when I see what is playing on the track. About four years ago, sitting by the garden wall, I swore that I had seen the masked face of a polecat. It was a fleeting glimpse and by the time I had called Jack over it had vanished. In the absence of any other sightings, I don't think anyone really believed me and I'd also started to question my own memory. Here on the track, complete with masked face, black paws and long, mustelid's body was a polecat, or at the very least a polecat-ferret, a hybrid between a wild polecat and a domesticated ferret. Polecats are native to the UK but were persecuted almost to extinction by the early 20th century. They began to recover, expanding their range, but North Lincolnshire is on the edge of their distribution so it's very unusual to see them here. However, when they have been sighted in the region, more than 95 per cent of the sightings

have been verified as 'true' polecats rather than hybrids, so it is considered an area containing 'pure' polecats. Combining this information with some telltale features, although we can't be certain, it is not unreasonable to think that the animal I saw on the track was a true polecat. Polecats are members of the mustelid family, related to badgers, stoats and weasels. They dine on rabbits, rats and voles and although they will take birds and eggs, their ability to control rat numbers means that their presence results in fewer animals that will predate on the chicks and eggs of ground-nesting birds.

There is also some evidence to suggest that in areas where polecats are present, they drive out the American mink, an invasive and highly destructive predator that is credited in part with the collapse of water vole populations. It's wonderful to see the return of a canny native predator back to the woodlands and hedgerows of the countryside where it belongs.

* * * * *

The track is the main connecting artery running through the farm. It runs behind the house and borders the bottom end of Benard's Field and Lone Pasture leading to the entrance to Fox Cover with The Park running along the other side. It is lined on both sides by hedgerows of hawthorn, blackthorn, field maple, wild privet, rose and elder. Tangles of brambles and wild flowers billow out from them forming a deep thicket and it is punctuated at various points by small woodland copses. It is so rich with life that the hedgerow sings with birds and hums with the vibrations of tiny wings all summer long. Grassy tunnels along the base of the hedgerow delicately pick out pathways through the thorny scrub and they are used by a whole host of animals that make their home at the heart of the farm.

It's probably no surprise that we happened to see the polecat here along the track. One of its most prolific residents forms the biggest part of a polecat's preferred diet. We have a huge population of rabbits here on the farm and they are concentrated in large numbers in this area around the house where we sit on an island of slightly sandier soil that is much easier to dig compared with the clay that dominates the rest of the farm. They particularly love to sunbathe on the track, so much so that it is affectionately known as 'rabbit alley', as there are always at least a dozen rabbits there at any one time. At night, a visit to The Park with an infrared camera reveals hundreds of them grazing on the grass and meadow flowers that grow there. Of course, they have no respect for boundaries, and our garden is also fair game, making it extremely difficult to grow anything without netting as they make light work of tender shoots, and I'm discovering that very little is unpalatable to rabbits. Despite these minor inconveniences, it's impossible not to be enchanted by the rabbits that are a constant and enduring presence. Thoroughly living up to their fecund reputation, from spring well into late summer, baby rabbits are produced with astonishing efficiency. I defy anyone not to melt at the sight of a newly minted clutch of baby bunnies nibbling a patch of clover in the lawn, their little ears short and round, and a snowy white tail like a powder puff flashing with each hop. They are a reliable subject if I want to sketch and sitting in the warm sun of a summer afternoon on the track surrounded by birdsong is perfection.

The seasonal succession of plants has once again moved on and the verges are full of clover and bird's-foot trefoil that grows in huge yellow swathes. Vetchlings curl their searching tendrils around blades of grass, thrusting their little purple flowers skywards as the leaves unfurl in pairs climbing the stem like the rungs of a ladder. Yarrow is also flowering. Its delicate white umbels are tinged with pink and they hover over the sward like candyfloss. I sit 20 metres (66 foot) or so from the rabbits and although one or two dart under the hedge, there are six or seven that nonchalantly ignore my quiet presence and carry on nibbling away, their lips and febrile noses in constant, twitchy motion. They vary in size and I think there must be kits from at least two of this year's litters among them. It's a good exercise in proportion and what makes an animal that essentially looks exactly the same as another inherently appear to be an infant. The littlest, with its outsized, rounded head and large brown eyes would fit in the palm of my hand. A big buck stretches in the sun and as they forget I'm there a few more rabbits emerge from the safety of the hedge. I try to capture the shape of their bodies as they run – their backs are a perfectly symmetrical curved bowl shape ending in that perfect little tail that creates satisfying balance in their form. I'm struck by how different they are in terms of movement, shape and behaviour from hares, despite their superficial similarities. The time slips by and eventually I have to drag myself away and head back home. I disturb a wood pigeon and it clatters out of the tree chaotically with the noise and drama that only a pigeon seems to be able to create. I look back over my shoulder and the track is completely empty.

August

The little grebe chicks have finally hatched. Five downy balls of black fluff with narrow stripes streaking down their heads like seams of gold. It's actually quite difficult to ascertain how many chicks there are. They shelter snugly under the wings of their parents, and every so often another seems to materialize from what looks like an impossibly small space, as though plucked from Mary Poppins' bag. They are understandably very nervous – it's unlikely that all five chicks will fledge – and I try to make myself inconspicuous as far away as I can get while keeping them in view with the binoculars. I end up settling on the mound at the edge of the ponds.

I am surrounded by the chirping voices of crickets and grasshoppers, singing at different pitches and creating one long, continuously vibrating chord. A pair of grasshoppers is lined up behind one another on a blade of grass. One of them has lost a hind leg but still enthusiastically draws its remaining leg against its rigid wing case like a bow over the strings of a violin, producing half the song of its neighbour. In contrast, crickets produce their song using only their hind legs and my mind wanders down a rabbit hole wondering about one-legged crickets – do they vibrate their remaining leg

against a phantom limb and wonder why they have been silenced? The song is surprisingly complex, and what sounds to me like simple vibrations convey a multitude of messages to their fellow hoppers, from romantic overtures to defensive threats and danger warnings. A large cricket lands on my knee – it has neon green flashes on its legs and a C-shaped neon curve on its flank like a Nike tick. It is a Roesel's bush-cricket. Its body is plated with chitinous armour and it waves around long, elegant antennae that protrude from the top of its head. It is not a native species to the UK but was first recorded in England in the mid-19th century. Once only found in the south of the country, they are steadily spreading as climate change leads to warmer weather, slowly but surely edging the limits of their distribution further north. In a swift motion too fast for my eyes to decipher it extends its powerful hind legs and flicks back into the long grass.

A grey heron and a pair of little egrets are browsing at the edge of the far pond. There is an abundance of pond snails littering the sandy bed as though they have been cast there carelessly. The largest of them, the great pond snail, has a long, sharply pointed spiral shell and is often walking on the ceiling of its aquatic world, using the surface tension to adhere its muscular foot to the underside of the water surface. They no doubt make a tasty snack, but the grebe chicks would also be easy targets for the large grey heron, and its continuous presence at the ponds poses an ominous threat. It is an impressive bird with long, sturdy legs that lift its body away from the water like stilts. Its wings appear to be wrapped around it like a shawl edged with light grey fronds slung over its shoulders, and the black cap on its head terminates in long streamers that trail behind it in the breeze. Its small, pale eyes are sharp and quietly penetrating but it is the dagger-like beak that sends a chill down the spine. Powerful jabs into the water dispatch whatever unfortunate prey it is stalking but this can provide little more than an appetizer for such a large bird. When it takes off, lifting into the air noiselessly on long, arched wings, it folds its long neck into a tight U-bend, circling the ponds a few times before disappearing over the tree tops.

Satisfied with my sketches I head for home and every footstep through the long grass sends up a shower of crickets and grasshoppers. The great burnet is in flower and blood-red pompoms float among the feathery grasses. I pass a bare patch of dusty soil and see a gathering of flying ants, their fat black bodies denser and larger than those of their wingless sisters. The swarms leaving the nests at this time of year consist of new queens and males in search of a mate. Although they emerge from the nest together, their destinies are entirely different. The queens, once mated, will land and shed their cumbersome wings as they search for a suitable nesting site to start a colony of their own. The males are not so fortunate. Once they have fertilized the new queens, their role is complete, and they will die shortly after mating. The abundance of ants during these swarming events provides food for many different species.

* * * * *

It's mid-August and there is once again a sense of shifting foundations. The days are still warm and long but autumn is hustling impatiently in the wings. The hawthorn flowers have transformed into swollen green berries that are just beginning to blush and they hang from lichen-encrusted branches in large clusters. Unripe green crab apples cling tightly to their boughs as the August sunshine coaxes them to sweeten and young green elderberries form sprays where there were once flamboyant umbels that smelled like honey. The riotous blackthorn carnival of early spring has failed to yield an abundance of fruit. Here and there shy sloes peek out from among the leaves, their coats frosted like breath on a cold window pane. The insects seemed slow to awaken this year and I wonder whether the blackthorn flowers had given up before they arrived.

Tall stands of rosebay willowherb line the hedgerows and a flush of pink stretches across the landscape. Cerise flowers are chased up the stem by feathery down that escapes like wisps of smoke. It is the favourite food plant of the elephant hawk moth caterpillar and I spend more time than is healthy searching for them but so far have had no success.

Many of this year's juvenile birds are around, fledged from their parents' care and ready to face the oncoming change of seasons independently. Their youth is visible in their plumage – similar to their parents but just different enough to make you question your identification of them – at least to my inexperienced eyes. It seems to have been

a good year for green woodpeckers and there are several young birds around the house, their plumage dusted with freckles that disappear in adulthood. We're used to hearing their yaffling call, jarring and loud, carrying across the farm but rarely catch sight of them. These younger birds are brave and numerous, and after loudly announcing their presence with a raucous laugh, they swoop between trees with their distinctive undulating flight. Green woodpeckers like to eat ants, using their strong beaks to break into nests, and they thrive in a habitat that can offer them a combination of mature trees and closely cropped grass. It's an example of why low densities of grazing animals are vital as part of a complex, dynamic ecosystem.

Unripe green crab apples cling tightly to their boughs as the August sunshine coaxes them to sweeten and young green elderberries form sprays where there were once flamboyant umbels that smelled like honey.

It's showery this afternoon so instead of heading out, I retrieve the memory card from one of the trail cameras I had left on the track and, with a hot mug of coffee, I embark on some wildlife watching from the comfort of my office. Unsurprisingly, there are hours and hours of rabbit footage, both day and night. The occasional hare lopes down the track and foxes are regular visitors. On sunny afternoons, blackbirds diligently search for worms in the grassy strip that runs down the middle of the track. Occasionally a fat moth triggers the sensor and once or twice an unsuspecting pair of legs in wellies is caught unawares. At one point, a kestrel swoops right in front of the camera and I suspect that it lands on the post to which the camera is attached. Slowing the film down, the footage

is amazing – the kestrel's yellow-rimmed eyes look straight into the lens, wings outstretched in perfect symmetry and black-tipped tail fanned out like a rudder slowing it down as it comes into land. Clutched in one bright yellow claw is a field vole.

If ever there was a symbol of the devastating loss of wildlife we have suffered in our country, it is encapsulated in the story of the hedgehog. Once they could be found snuffling for slugs and worms under every hedgerow, ubiquitous and common, the prickly symbol of the countryside. We love our hedgehogs, but this love has not been enough to sustain them, and the hedgehog is now at risk of complete extinction. Wildness has been driven out of our country, relegated to the margins and what is left remains in isolated fragments. We have broken up the networks of connectivity that hedgehogs need to sustain their nocturnal wanderings with tarmac, impenetrable garden boundaries and ever-enlarging agricultural fields. Pesticides and cultivation have led to a catastrophic decline in their prey and competition for resources has left them vulnerable to predation. We try to exonerate ourselves by blaming the decline on a burgeoning badger population, badgers being the only predator undeterred by the hedgehog's spines. When it tries to curl into a tight ball, the badger's long claws can prise it apart, giving it access to the hedgehog's soft, vulnerable underbelly. But hedgehog numbers are in free fall even where badgers are absent. Where the habitat is rich and intact with plenty of food, the two species have been shown to live alongside one another happily. The numbers are hard to ascertain, but is estimated that the UK population now numbers around 800,000 hogs, and as many 300,000 are killed on the road each year – their defensive instinct to curl up into a tight, prickly ball is their undoing when faced with a four wheeled foe. The situation is bleak.

Fortunately, hedgehogs are still clinging on here. The dense thorny scrub alongside the track provides them with protection and as night falls they emerge, led by their noses in search of juicy morsels. The trail camera switches from daylight mode, capturing shadowy images that are devoid of colour. Small, bright eyes nestle like berries in the soft fur of their face that morphs into keratinous quills, dark at the base and fading to blonde. The rotund ball of prickles is elevated from the ground by dark little legs, and they are surprisingly agile as they forage, their senses alerted to the dangers that may lurk around every corner.

I come to the end of the footage and it's still raining but I need to get outside. I put on my wellies and let the warm summer rain freshen my lungs and dampen my hair as it nourishes the dry soils.

* * * * *

Gentle breezes push soft
ripples across the surface
of the pond like folds in
fabric and the low, swollen
sun lights them with a warm,
livid glow. Now joined by this
year's offspring, swallows that
bred in the local area (but sadly
not in our barn) gather in larger
numbers. They skim the surface
for unsuspecting insects that skate
on the surface tension. Occasionally
they graze the surface, splashing
their white bellies into the water
that licks their feathers clean.

Wild roses, their indigestible
seeds planted across the farm
by the many animals and birds
that enjoy their fruits, appear
in disorganized tangles. Long
whips form thorny arches studded with
orange hips. Alongside them, another strange structure nestles
between the thorns. Raspberry red, it looks like a soft mass of
mossy, feather-like fronds. It is a robin's pincushion. The presence
of an egg, laid into a leaf bud by an amber-legged wasp, *Diplolepis
rosae*, performs a chemical magic trick that instructs the bud to
develop into this intricate structure that will nurse the wasp's
larvae through the winter. The 'robin' in its name refers not to the
bird but to a wood sprite, a more ancient meaning of the word.

The heavy air feels languid and lazy. I've come out to sketch
in the late sun but I'm struggling to motivate myself. Elvis and
Claude are with me and they seem keen to get home too. Every

time it looks like I'm preparing to leave, they dart ahead, extending their leads to the maximum, then look at me impatiently, wearily wandering back when they realize I'm not ready yet. Eventually I give in, and we walk along the mown path through the newly planted woodland at the edge of Fox Cover. The dogs are delighted and bound along the path.

Elvis stops suddenly a little way ahead, his head tilted. As I catch him up, I spot what had captured his attention. A hole in the ground around the size of a football is littered with the dead bodies of red-tailed bumblebees. A lone bee floats around aimlessly, her jet black, furry body dipped in molten amber. The nest has been excavated by a hungry badger, raiding its nectar stores and eating the juicy larvae developing in brood cells. Red-tailed bumblebees nest underground in cavities, often using abandoned rodent burrows. Although not their usual diet, badgers are opportunistic hunters, and its strong claws would have made light work of excavating the nest.

As the lonely bee buzzes off, Elvis is satisfied with his investigation and trots off after Claude in the direction of home.

Later that evening, Jack has gone to play tennis with some friends and I'm sitting with the dogs about to see if I can find anything to watch on TV. A retching sound coming from behind the sofa alerts me to the fact that Claude is being sick. I leap up in an attempt to move him off the carpet and onto the hard floor in the corridor as a means of damage limitation, but as I get close, he suddenly loses his balance and is rolling around unable to get up. I've never seen anything like this before and start to panic. I ring the vet who says he will meet me at the practice. I manage to get Claude to stop rolling and he just lies on the floor panting. I get a blanket to make him more comfortable in the car. He manages to trot after me, but I can see he's still struggling to balance, swaying like a drunk as he follows me outside. This little dog never leaves our side. He loves coming with us whenever we head out in the car, and even in his current state he seems to be cheered that we're going out for a ride, but the poor thing hates the vet. His experience of this place up to now is being poked and prodded or jabbed with needles. Even now, he doesn't want to go inside, and I can feel his small body shivering as I take him in. He has stopped being sick but he's still wobbly and drooling continuously. The vet's verdict is that he has most likely ingested some kind of poison, possibly an insecticide. I am incredulous. What? How? We use no pesticides at all on the land and don't store anything like that anywhere on the farm. I can't understand how this could have happened – he just wouldn't have access to anything like it. The vet reassures me. They will give him some activated charcoal and put him on a drip which should do the trick. A nurse is on the way to look after him through the night. He whimpers as I leave but I cheerfully tell him I'll see him in the morning.

In the morning, the vet rings me at 8 am. Claude passed away overnight. We are all inconsolable. I am consumed by guilt because I am the one who took him out the night before. I must have taken my eyes off him for a split second at the wrong time. I feel terrible that I didn't anticipate this outcome and stay to comfort him at the vets. I can't bear the thought of him being alone and frightened. Claude was our first family dog. Bright, bold and full of joy, he was a one-off. We all loved Claude, and he loved us, but he definitely had a favourite. He was utterly devoted to Jack. All day long he followed him around like a little black shadow. Wherever Jack went, Claude followed. He was never meant to belong to Jack but for some reason, an unbreakable bond formed between them, and Jack is completely devastated by Claude's sudden death. I have to admit, I never fully understood the terrible feeling of losing a much-loved animal until now. He was part of our family, and we all feel his absence with the intensity of a raw, angry wound. I keep thinking I can hear the tinkling sound his collar made and then the shock hits me all over again. Poor Elvis is confused and keeps looking quizzically at Claude's empty bed. He's quiet and subdued, mirroring the mood engulfing the rest of the family.

We bury Claude's small body under an oak tree, the same tree that also watches over my mum's ashes. The vet could shed no more light on the mystery poison. Our best guess is that he ate some grass that was contaminated by ergot, a psychoactive fungus that infects the florets of flowering grasses and can be found at this time of year, an innocuous fruiting body hiding away in the ears of rye grasses. I doubt we'll ever know for sure.

September

The buzzard, all heft and swagger while clumsily hunting for worms among sparse grassy pastures, transforms into a creature of effortless grace as it circles and eddies on the thermals that hold it aloft high above the farm. Its prehistoric banshee wails are an eerie reminder of its reptilian ancestry and have become ubiquitous in every county in the UK.

It's early September and the last embers of summer still valiantly warm the ground, giving the grasses and saplings a late flush of growth in the September rains, but it's clear that autumn has already started her relentless march. The brambles have fruited and are now intent on growth. Searching tendrils stretch across the paths like blind fingers exploring their surroundings. The morning dew has settled jewel-like on the ground and temporarily illuminated the millions of cobwebs that seem to create an endless network of ephemeral threads connecting every blade of grass; a fleeting glimpse of a shimmering blanket in the morning sun.

There's rarely a day that we don't see a buzzard somewhere on the farm and among them is a pair that breed here every year in an unwieldy jumble of a nest wedged firmly in the fork of an oak tree at the edge of the farm. The female is the bigger of the pair, and her freckled plumage is distinctly paler than any other buzzard we've seen around here, so she is easy to identify. This morning she's perched on a fence post, an ideal vantage point from which to hunt. Buzzards are opportunists, and the majority of her diet will be made up of small mammals, but she'll also take amphibians, carrion, birds and invertebrates. We almost lost this raptor from our skies. Suffering heavy persecution during Victorian times due to

what turned out to be an incorrect assumption about their impact on game birds, buzzard numbers had just started to recover when the outbreak of myxomatosis decimated the rabbit population and obliterated an important food source. At the same time, pesticides such as DDT percolated through the food chain, weakening the eggshells of breeding birds and emptying the skies of their song. The recovery of the buzzard to become the most common raptor in the UK is an incredible conservation success. As ever where nature collides with the interests of humans, the proliferation of buzzards sits uncomfortably with some. Our innate instinct to be in control and to frame nature as an adversary often seems to override what the evidence is telling us. As is almost always the case, recovery of habitat and restoration of functioning ecosystems with apex predators would be a far easier and more ecologically sound way to re-establish balance in the natural world.

The hulking female sits nonchalantly on her post, unconcerned by my presence as I spy on her through my binoculars to capture her form as best I can in pencil on paper. Buzzards are often compared unfavourably to their raptorial cousins and the name 'buzzard' derives from an old French word, *buisart*, which translates as 'inferior hawk'. If you are ever fortunate enough to catch a glimpse of a goshawk materialize from the shadows with the precision and force of a stealth fighter jet, expertly navigating dense woodland to seize its prey before disappearing like an otherworldly killing machine, it's an awe-inspiring sight. In comparison, observing a buzzard hopping clumsily as it attempts to rouse worms from their subterranean hiding spots seems rather comical. However, spend a little time in their company and it doesn't take long to develop a healthy respect for these resourceful birds. The sheer size of the female is impressive as she opens her broad wings to reveal delicately mottled covert feathers yielding to black tipped, lightly barred primaries that separate in flight to look like fingers.

Something has caught her attention and she glides off her perch, plopping down before defying gravity to take off again, the tail of an unfortunate rat dangling limply from her scaled talons.

* * * * *

The summer is unwilling to relinquish her hold on the farm and hazy sunshine reflects off the mirror surface of the ponds. The air feels thick and hot, and the sound of grasshoppers and crickets in the long grass is penetrating and loud. Orb weaver spiders levitate between blades of grass as they traverse the invisible pathways they have woven in search of prey. Always late to the party, there are hundreds of common darter dragonflies paired up, the male jealously guarding the female from rival males. Grasping the base of her head in the claspers on his red abdomen, the pair rise and fall rhythmically, an egg being laid each time the female dips the tip of her body delicately onto the surface of the water. The stridulations of crickets and grasshoppers provide a background hum to the beat of a percussive snare as her wings vibrate against the vegetation when she dips to lay an egg.

Away from the ponds, the entire field appears to be quivering. A mass emergence of crane flies, unsuppressed by insecticides, has enveloped the farm. A tangle of improbably long legs and inadequate looking wings, they appear like some kind of evolutionary blip as they bumble along the ground inelegantly, seemingly unsure what to do with their dangly appendages. A creature that spends most of its life in larval form, these adult crane flies will have one thing on their mind, as they live just long enough to breed before dying. In the meantime, their emergence will provide a feeding bonanza for a multitude of predatory insects, mammals, amphibians and birds, including swallows and martins who are currently fuelling up for their impending migrations. The crane fly larvae, known as leatherjackets, are also ecologically important. As well as providing a food source, they are detritus feeders, breaking down organic matter into nutrients and creating micro-environments for other creatures. They also feed on the roots of dominant grasses, creating clearings in which other seeds can germinate, helping to create diverse, flower-rich grassland.

Enjoying the warmth of the late summer sun, I settle myself down and try to become a part of the landscape as I wait to see what emerges. It's a quiet afternoon and after sketching a couple of sun-drunk wood pigeons I'm about to pack up when I spot a hare in the distance. After nonchalantly nibbling on a few shoots, it begins loping along one of the many well-worn animal tracks that snake across the farm like a network of arteries.

Hopping towards me on huge hind feet and held aloft on legs like stilts that look out of proportion with the rest of its body, it's not hard to see where its magical powers lie. Built for speed and agility, those powerful legs are the hare's only means of defence. Without a burrow to escape to, the ability to accelerate and suddenly change direction are the secret weapons of the brown hare. I once watched a fox stealthily approach a hare across open ground and as it got closer, I couldn't understand why the hare was still hanging around. As the fox got closer, rather than make a run for it, the hare performed some kind of aerial gymnastics, kicking its powerful legs into the air before turning its attention back to the patch of grass it had been nibbling. Amazingly, the fox just trotted

on by without a second glance. I wondered if the hare had been signalling to the fox of the power in those hind legs and whether the fox knew from bitter experience that it had little chance of making a meal of a hare with such impressive assets. This behaviour would have allowed both animals to conserve precious energy rather than engage in a futile game of chase.

The hare is now close enough to sketch without the need for binoculars, and I try to move as little as possible. Naturally wary, it is constantly alert. Black-tipped, oversized ears look like elongated satellite dishes, capturing any small vibration that might signal danger. The hare's nose and cheeks are in constant motion, continuously tasting the air and nibbling at the grass and the result is a comical array of eccentric facial expressions which seem at odds with the mythical aura that surrounds this beautiful animal.

I feel like I've been holding my breath for the last few minutes, but seemingly unconcerned by my presence, something else captures the hare's attention. Momentarily, it pins its ears back and crouches lower before deciding to dart off into a thicket of brambles at the foot of a wayward hedge.

October

October has arrived and early autumn rains
have drenched the thirsty ground. Pools
have started to form across the farm, the clay
soils cradling the water as it falls from grey
clouds that hang low and heavy in the sky. The
trees and hedgerows have yet to start their annual
moult in earnest, but the palette has begun to
change, and rich golds and reds have started to appear like gilding
among the green. Haws and hips weigh heavily on branches,
waiting for the winter migrants to arrive in search of this year's
berries. Hedge bindweed still clambers through the undergrowth
embracing the brambles in its curling tendrils as its white trumpets
open like parasols, loudly announcing the presence of nectar to
passing pollinators. Ivy, with its contrarian habit, is just coming
into flower as most other plants have given up, lime-green blooms
held out on sturdy stalks like celestial bodies among the waxy
leaves. This is a vital pollen source for late-flying insects. A dozen
red admirals flutter among the flowers and a garden spider, its
bulbous abdomen painted with a delicate white cross, sits at the
centre of its round web stretching across the leaves.

There is a brief hiatus in the wet weather this morning, so I
head up the farm to be alone with my thoughts. Perhaps it is the
change of seasons and diminishing light, but I've been feeling a
bit low recently. The state of nature report has just been published
and yet again it makes grim reading. A collaborative report by
60 conservation agencies, it collates data from across the UK and
paints a bleak picture of the health of our wildlife. It finds that

one in six species in the UK is at risk of being lost and 43 per cent of birds are now at risk of extinction, mainly due to human activity leading to habitat loss, diseases such as avian flu stemming from intensive factory farming conditions and climate change resulting from the burning of fossil fuels. And still we continue with our relentless assault on nature. The news is full of depressing stories: 'acres of ancient orchard to be cleared to make way for a new "green" bus route in Cambridge'; 'anglers in Wales petition for culling of fish-eating birds'; 'the government approves the development of a huge new oil and gas field in the North Sea'. In the lanes of North Lincolnshire, now that nesting season is over, the flails are at work reducing hedgerows to neat square blocks of ravaged twigs, spilling what few berries were produced across the roads. The lines of hedgerows surrounding the vast fields in our county have the potential to be a vital interconnected source of habitat for a huge variety of creatures, but it is another lost opportunity. For what? What would it cost to allow just the hedgerows to become a little more wild?

I'm so used to being surrounded by a constant background soundscape of birdsong here at home that I'm noticing increasingly a quietness elsewhere. Almost everywhere you go, even places that embody the quintessential English countryside, it is quiet. We have forgotten that as we gaze over rolling, sheep-grazed hills, studded with isolated trees and criss-crossed with ancient stone walls that there is something missing from the scene. And because we have forgotten, we don't see that something is wrong, and the destructive pattern is allowed to continue unabated.

Walking down the track, I open the trusty Merlin app on my phone. Although not perfect, this is an invaluable tool to any would-be birder. It listens to the birdsong and produces a neat list of the species producing it. I have found it incredibly helpful in learning to recognize different songs that felt completely

overwhelming at the start. I sit for a while and just listen, unthreading the individual voices from the tangle of noise. Within ten minutes, Merlin has recorded 23 different species including linnet, bullfinch, long-tailed tit, wren, robin, buzzard, blackcap, song thrush, chaffinch, jackdaw, chiffchaff, skylark and pied wagtail. I'm about to move on when another little voice joins the throng, high pitched and shrill like a squeaking wheel. It's not an uncommon bird. I've heard it often and once found the remnants of its complex, cup-shaped nest woven from moss, lichen and spiders' webs hidden among a thicket of ivy that embraced an old spruce tree, but I've barely ever seen it on the farm. Our smallest bird, a tiny goldcrest, flickers among the branches of an ash tree like a little flame. Goldcrests are commonly associated with coniferous forests but are widespread across the UK. They are insectivores and make the most of their diminutive size by hunting at the tips of tiny branches where heavier birds are unable to venture. Incredibly for a bird that weighs around the same as a 20-pence piece, our native population is joined by a large influx from Scandinavia in the autumn. It flits and scurries like a little mouse, constantly on the move, its lofty song sitting somewhere among the frequencies barely audible to our senses.

Above my head, a dozen or so barn swallows perch on telegraph wires strung over the track. It seems late for them to be here but it's still mild and our warming climate is altering and shifting the very foundations upon which the natural world rests.

* * * * *

Seasonal change is finally picking up some pace and the pale sun no longer has the strength to warm the chill in the October air. It's a bright, cold day. The ground is saturated from the recent rain and ephemeral pools glisten as they reflect the sunlight. The damp weather has coaxed fungal networks that are woven through the fabric of the land to fruit and toadstools of all shapes and sizes have erupted. Shaggy ink caps cluster together like a congregation, their bell-shaped pilei resembling woolly wigs before they dissolve into an oozing black slick. Elsewhere, hare's foot ink caps, weeping widows and milky cone caps all peak shyly through the wet grass.

A lone chiffchaff still sings in the wood at the end of the track but many of the warblers that bred here over the summer have now gone, compelled by an ancient and primal urge to fly south to seek milder temperatures over winter. They are replaced by other species that have started to arrive now from the colder northern reaches where the winter is frozen and hostile. As the seasons change, millions of birds across 250 different species migrate to our shores. Some, such as fieldfares and redwings, only appear during the winter, but many join existing breeding populations, swelling their numbers. The factors that trigger these astonishing journeys aren't fully understood, but it is thought that changes in day length, food availability and temperatures all play a part. Back in the days when it was considered acceptable to keep birds in cages, it was well documented that migratory birds such as robins would become restless during the autumn, fluttering in the southerly corners of their enclosures, unable to suppress the intrinsic urge to migrate despite their imprisonment.

On the ponds today is a bevy of returning migrants. Elegant white birds with long, slender necks and sunshine yellow beaks tipped with black as though they have been dipped in a pot of ink. The juveniles among them are still muddied with their soft, grey plumage, a monochrome version of their parents as the yellow on their beaks is yet to appear. Whooper swans are known in Japan as Angels of Winter. Wild and untamed, these birds have travelled here from Iceland. It's likely that they are en route to the estuaries and wetlands where they will spend the winter, just pausing a while to rest at our ponds. They stay for a few hours, floating noiselessly on the glassy surface of the water, barely causing it to ripple as they preen their feathers. Eventually the time comes for them to depart, and they lift from the water like a single body, soft bugle calls volleying between them as they continue their onward journey.

A house martin, often among the last of the migrating birds to leave, darts over the water, dipping its white belly into the wake

left by the swans as it skims insects from the surface. It disappears over the hedge, its erratic, fluttery flight looking breathtakingly inadequate to carry it the long distances it has to travel.

* * * * *

It's a perfect day to be outside on the farm, clear and still. I love the quality of the autumn sunlight. Lacking the brash golden confidence of summer, the damp light gently calms every colour it touches and there is something soothing about gazing out over the fields on a day like this. We still haven't had a hard frost yet and there are little pockets of blue where borage is still in flower. There hasn't been a crop of borage on the farm for at least 15 years, but this is a persistent little plant. Despite attempts to beat it into submission for more than a decade, it valiantly persisted every year, and now left to its own devices it flourishes at the top end of Lone Pasture, offering up its pretty blue flowers to the bees who greedily accept. Borage has a long flowering season and is useful in filling the 'nectar gap' for insects at the height of summer but it has usually turned to seed by now. There are disturbing signs everywhere that the seasons are out of kilter with the normal order of things, and in the garden, seeds still encased in their seed heads have been confused into germinating by the mild, damp weather.

Elsewhere, the thistles that we were able to leave on the farm have gone to seed. Thistles are pioneer plants, and we have a good selection of them, from delicate creeping thistle to the more stately spear variety. Relishing the unloved and forgotten, they can eke out a living from the thinnest of soils, quickly establishing an army of tall stems bearing weapons in the form of spindly needles. As we discovered earlier this year, their plucky and tenacious character isn't always considered an endearing trait, and the sight of thistles marching across wild areas has been met with some dismay and disapproval. Despite this fearsome reputation, thistles are an important food source for a huge variety of species. A myriad of pollinators, including painted lady butterflies, are famous for their love of creeping thistle, and if you look a little closer you might see small translucent pathways etched onto the leaves, a sign that a mining insect is living inside the leaves themselves.

Unlike the borage, the feathery purple thistle flowers have completed their transformation to seed, and every stem is capped by a globe bursting with soft down. Brown and brittle, the skeletal remains of this year's crop looks spiky and hostile, but today we are rewarded with another species enjoying the abundance of thistles on the farm.

Goldfinches are sociable little birds, and once the breeding season has finished, they come together to form large flocks. Their twinkling chatter is very distinctive and gave rise to the beautifully apt collective noun: a charm of goldfinches, derived from the old English term c'irm, which describes the blended clamour of many tinkling voices.

A huge flock of goldfinches is gorging on the thistle seeds. I think there must be more than 150 birds in this group, sturdy beaks perfectly designed for freeing hundreds of seeds and clouds of down. Individually, the birds are real beauties. Little sprites, faces masked in ruby red, they occasionally reveal a flash of golden yellow on their wings. Collectively, they are mesmerizing. The field quivers as they go about their business and occasionally the whole flock lifts like a blanket, murmurating in perfect coordination until the cloak gently lands on a fresh patch of thistles. I can't help but feel that the ubiquity of goldfinches has led to us undervaluing these charming little birds.

As for the thistles, they will become less dominant as the scrub matures and the natural succession progresses beyond these early pioneers claiming the bare soil as their own. For now, I'm content to revel in their glorious untidiness and the riches that they bear.

November

The winter thrushes have arrived in abundance. With the help of easterly winds, many thousands of fieldfares, redwings and blackbirds have made their way to our shores from Scandinavia to join their resident cousins. Ganging together in a huge riotous mob, flocks of thrushes numbering well into the hundreds have descended on the hedgerows in search of berries.

I am a little obsessed with hedgerows. Old maps of the farm show that where there are now two enormous fields, both around 1.6km (1 mile) long, there was once a patchwork of smaller pastures separated by hedgerows. The loss of these field boundaries up and down the country has been a tragedy for our wildlife. Although they are a human construct, hedgerows are the best proxy we have for another lost ecosystem – messy, scrubby pasture, rich with hawthorn, elder, blackthorn and bramble, which is vital habitat for many species.

The 10 kilometres (6 miles) or so of hedgerow that we have remaining across the farm has largely been left untouched for the past ten years. The result is a dense, tangled mixture of scrubby, thorny vegetation interspersed with the odd oak or field maple, flanked at the base by a skirt of grasses, bramble and marginal wild flowers. In the spring, it is cloaked in fragrant blossoms, each species taking its turn to flower like a well-disciplined orchestra, and the air around it hums with the sound of beating wings. By autumn, the soft blossoms have given up their fruits and every branch is festooned with jewels. This is the treasure that the thrushes have travelled all this way to find.

It's late afternoon by the time I manage to get outside today and a barn owl is already gliding across the field. The thrushes have not yet roosted, and the hedge is quivering with the movement of hundreds of birds within the confines of its branches. The constant chatter of fieldfares fills the air as they browse the smorgasbord of berries on offer. A few starlings have joined them, seeking the protection to be found in large numbers but the majority of them today are thrushes, their familiar body shape betraying their shared ancestry.

Fieldfares are larger than a blackbird and I think there must be well over 300 of them in this particular flock. They are truly striking, with a cool, blue-grey head contrasting with the warmth of their chestnut wings, and a breast speckled with darts that instantly identifies them as a member of the thrush family. Occasional squabbles break out with a shrill 'chak-chak-chak', but the overall impression is one of unity. The hedgerow and its inhabitants is a single organism, breathing and shuddering as one.

Further down towards the village I can see that the thrushes have already stripped virtually every berry from the hawthorn. The bare skeleton, devoid of all colour, looks stark against the sky but the removal of its ruby-red clothing has revealed yet more secrets. Old nests of all shapes and sizes, from dense little balls

of moss to loose, sprawling, twiggy affairs, are littered throughout the branches. When spring arrives, these old hedgerows will once again become a nursery for a new generation of chicks, but by then the fieldfares will be gone from our island, building nests of their own in faraway lands.

* * * * *

The landscape has undergone a dramatic metamorphosis. Verdant greens are fading to gold. For now, the leaves still cling to their branches, and from a distance the hedgerows are breathtakingly beautiful. Yellows and ochres rub shoulders with rich coppers and burnished bronzes. The leaves of the spindle trees that nestle among the hawthorns glow with the intensity of molten metal. At the bottom end of Benard's Field, the self-set silver birches stand at over 3 metres (10 foot) tall, their papery leaves whispering to one another in raspy voices as the wind whips between them. The seeds that gave rise to these trees blew across the field only a couple of years ago. They are pioneers, colonizing newly bare soil and racing skywards with vigorous urgency. At their feet, small but perfectly formed oaks are growing steadily. They are the hare and tortoise of the arboreal world, and as the landscape matures, the giant oaks will one day overshadow these birches.

A ring ouzel has been recorded on the farm for the first time and I've come over to Church Wood to see if I can catch sight of one. Resembling a blackbird, but sporting a white crescent emblazoned across its chest, ring ouzels are members of the thrush family. Unlike their cousins that arrived on the farm over the past few weeks, the ring ouzels are likely passing through before leaving our shores for the mountains of north-west Africa. A bird of the uplands, during the breeding season, they inhabit open moorlands and rocky crags at high altitudes in Scotland and Northern England.

Scouring the branches for the source of the hollow, sad whistle, I catch sight of the bullfinch. The coral-pink breast is vibrant and loud, and he sits like a Christmas bauble among the branches.

At one end of Church Wood, nestled in a sunny glade studded with hawthorn and hazel, is a hidden circular pond. Goat willows rooted into its banks lean over and peer into the water, and brambles have run riot, barbed whips catching on my coat as I brush past. A cluster of bulrushes has gone to seed, and I can't resist the urge to run my fingers over the velvety soft flowerhead, which sits like a skewered sausage on the tall stems. I dig my thumbnail into the velvet and plumes of pillowy down tumble out, releasing thousands of tiny seeds that are carried away as the slightest breeze catches the feathery cloud. I sit down on the damp bank and listen to the birdsong that fills the scrub. I'm getting better at recognizing some of the calls and I can hear the piping whistle of a bullfinch among the clamour of the fieldfares, redwings, blackbirds and robins. Scouring the branches for the source of the hollow, sad whistle, I catch sight of the bullfinch. The coral-pink breast is vibrant and loud, and he sits like a Christmas bauble among the branches. I stay for a while, enjoying the tranquility, when the Merlin app picks up a couple of notes that it identifies as a ring ouzel. It's fleeting, and I certainly couldn't claim to have heard it

myself, but I replay the recording. The little volley of 'crrk-chik-chik' calls sounds tantalizingly like a ring ouzel, but I don't hear it again and I don't catch sight of it, so I park the record firmly in the 'maybe' pile.

On the way back home across the wet field, I keep an eye open for another elusive bird that has spent the winter in the wet marshy grasses on the farm. The jack snipe is smaller and rarer than the common snipe. Secretive birds that overwinter in the UK, they hide in thick vegetation in marshy wetland, the golden stripes on their backs helping them to blend in among the thatch of grasses that

line the water's edge. I've seen films of them feeding, probing their long beaks into the wet mud, bobbing up and down as they feed, but the most I usually see of them is a fleeting glimpse in flight. Unlike common snipe, which flush as soon as they detect your footsteps nearby, jack snipe hunker down and disappear into the grasses. They are incredibly difficult to spot as a result and any that I passed today have remained hidden and undetected.

The news is full of a storm that is heading our way, bringing with it gale-force winds and torrents of rain. Sure enough, we are kept awake by ferocious wind that batters against our windows, angrily ripping off roof tiles and tearing down branches in its wild temper. The next morning, once the tempest has passed, the lane is covered in a blanket of golden leaves and the peak of the autumn display has disappeared with the storm.

* * * * *

One of my favourite winter arrivals on the farm is the woodcock. At some point in its evolutionary history, this wading bird discovered that its long beak was adept at probing for worms and other insects on the edges of woodland, and over many generations it adapted to exploit this rich habitat, abandoning the shores and mudflats of its distant ancestry.

On first appearance, the woodcock's face somehow seems distorted and the eyes out of proportion. In any painting I do, I always spend a disproportionate amount of time on the eyes. I know that getting them exactly right is crucial to the success of the whole painting – they bring it to life and any slight mistake in their shape, placement and proportions will give the animal a strange appearance immediately perceptible to even the most untrained observer, so attuned are we humans to the so-called 'windows of the soul'. Sketching a woodcock is giving me the highly uncomfortable urge to move the eyes closer to the beak as you would find in a more conventional bird. But the woodcock is not conventional bird.

If you spend all of your time beak down, rootling around in the soil for tasty morsels, your average forward- and sideways-facing eyes are going to leave you vulnerable to ambush from above and behind. As a result, evolution has gradually enlarged the woodcock's eyes and guided them up and backwards on its head, allowing it a panoramic view of its surroundings while it forages. In order to accommodate the eyes in this position, the ears have had to migrate forwards, ending up right next to its beak, and its brain was even rearranged to allow for this jumbled-up morphology.

If that's not enough to make you love this rotund little bird, legend has it that the thousands of woodcock migrating to join our resident population at the end of autumn carry on their backs tiny goldcrests, known in some parts as 'woodcock pilots'. It is thought that woodcock use the light of the November full moon to help guide their journey so, as with much local lore, there is probably a grain of truth in the story of the November 'woodcock moon'.

Despite being our most common wader, woodcock are experts in camouflage and it is very difficult to catch sight of them during the day. The little holes punctured into the mossy damp soil at the edge of the wood by a probing beak are reassuring signs that the woodcock are here and a clattering of branches in the bottom of a hedge heralds the disturbed bird's escape as it explodes out on chestnut, tawny wings in a rather erratic and haphazard manner.

December

Winter has arrived. After an abnormally warm and wet autumn, the temperatures have plummeted and everything is frozen. It feels like winter should do and the frost is finally taking the sting out of the nettles, ice crystals ravaging the tender leaves, while the heart of the plant hibernates underground. I can't remember the last time we had such a sustained period of frozen weather. When the temperatures hover around freezing, intermittent rain showers turn everything into a dirty, muddy slush. This year, it has been cold for long enough that the ponds have developed a covering of ice 7.5 centimetres (3 inches) thick, and a blanket of crystals has been delicately dusted across the landscape. The whitewash has softened all of the colours and given everything a cold blue hue.

The farm is eerily quiet. It feels as though all of nature is hiding away until the weather becomes more hospitable. I find it miraculous that anything can survive outside in these extreme temperatures. It's a perilous time for many species.

The frosted branches of the trees in the wood are bare and skeletal, and the ground is littered with discarded leaves, each one crystallized by the frozen air. It's such a stark difference from the verdant lushness of its summer incarnation, when the floor is splashed with golden sunlight, that it's hard to believe that the frozen heart of the woodland is still beating. But among the silvers and browns, clinging to slumbering tree trunks with sticky fingers, is an evergreen that provides a lifeline to many species at this time of year. Camouflaged by the frost, waxy green leaves and berries held out on little stalks arranged in starbursts wind themselves around trees. Ivy is an epiphyte. Although it relies on trees for support, it does not take nutrients from its host and causes no damage to it. Sadly, ivy is frequently mistaken for a malignant parasite and in the belief that it is mercilessly strangling its host trees, well-meaning woodland 'management' often involves the removal of this important native plant. In a neighbouring village, a small copse of mature woodland recently changed hands and the new owner decided to 'tidy' it up, removing the rich understory of messy scrub and rescuing the trees by slicing through ivy stems as thick as my wrist at the base of the trees. Every time we drive past it I have to avert my eyes. I can't bear to see the crispy brown remains of the ivy still clinging to the trees as it slowly decays or the neat grass that has replaced red campion, nettles and cuckoo pint.

In autumn, the ivy vibrates with bees, red admirals and hover flies enjoying the late source of nectar from the yellow-green, often overlooked, flowers. In winter, the berries are an important food source for a variety of insects and birds. Ivy supports more than 50 different species and there's one in particular that I've come to look for among the frozen leaves. Brimstone butterflies are one of the first to be spotted on the farm in spring, its lime-green wings resembling fresh leaves. Unlike other over-wintering butterflies that shelter from the cold in crevices in tree trunks or in the eaves of buildings, brimstones have a clever trick that enables them to nestle among the evergreen ivy all winter. Their blood, or haemolymph, contains polyhydroxy alcohols, a natural antifreeze that allows them to withstand freezing temperatures. Somewhere nestled among the

frozen leaves is likely to be a sleeping brimstone, its wings covered in ice crystals, waiting patiently for winter to pass. Today is not my day to find one, but I spy a pair of round amber eyes peering at me from a tendril of ivy that winds around an old fence lining the paddock as I return home. A pair of little owls lives in the hedgerow here. They are often perched on this fence and deposit small pellets that glisten with the wing cases of iridescent beetles all around the yard. The little owl has a small, round body topped with a flat, narrow head. It eyes me with what I interpret as scornful scepticism before deciding it has had enough of my presence and flying off across the paddock, its looping flight an easy way of identifying it from a distance.

* * * * *

It's raining again and it feels as though it will never stop. In the height of summer droughts, the ponds retreat dramatically, parching the soil and exposing the plants that like to be submerged, suffocating them in the warm air. Within a few short months they are overflowing into one another, the pathways that snake between them undecided as to whether they are land or lake. The rest of the farm is also wrestling with the same question and ephemeral pools have appeared everywhere. It's wet and boggy and the drowning vegetation offers a reminder of why we're not trying to establish a crop of wheat here. Although not conducive to growing arable crops, these transient bodies of water have an important role to play. Vernal pools will remain wet throughout the spring until the summer warmth returns and dries them out. Their temporary nature keeps them free of fish, so they provide the perfect habitat for amphibians to lay their eggs in, and many plants and invertebrates have adapted to exploit these important wetlands.

Another species enjoying the saturated conditions is the common snipe. The snipe is a wetland bird that visits the farm in large numbers over the winter and they are continuously darting out from the scrub. My footsteps have disturbed at least a dozen of them today and something about their jinking, jagged flight path and narrow, pointy wings reminds me of a bat as they fly off.

Church Wood is a copse of mixed native trees in the middle of the farm that Jack helped to plant as a teenager during the school Easter holidays almost 30 years ago. Although by no means a mature woodland, it's had long enough to develop some character and there is a good mix of large, healthy trees, sunlit glades, open scrub, dead wood that has been left to decay and a dose of natural regeneration too. In some places, the floor is covered in a dense carpet of fallen leaves and seed cases. On first appearances, the whole wood seems to have settled into its seasonal slumber, but the damp weather has awakened a whole kingdom. Entanglements of fungi are woven throughout the fabric of the wood, complex interactions with root systems creating a mycelial network fundamental to life. It's a mysterious world and we are only beginning to understand its importance and intricacies. The damp weather has encouraged the secretive fungi to reveal their fruiting bodies, which are the only visible evidence of their quiet existence that they are prepared to share with us.

Beefsteak fungus, wet and glistening like raw flesh, forms miniature steps clambering up the trunk of an oak, and a turkeytail with its colourful concentric circles resembling growth rings of a tree has taken residence on a rotting stump. The delightfully named witches' butter appears as a bright yellow eruption from the branches of an oak and fairy parachutes are suspended from the underside of another. Looking closer still, a cluster of tiny bonnet mushrooms barely more than a millimetre high protrudes from the junction between a trunk and stem. Meanwhile, green mosses

seep up tree trunks as if they have been dipped in ink, and delicate lichens in every shade of blue and green decorate branches like lace.

Lost in my own world and privately vowing to get better at identifying different mosses and fungi, I had failed to notice that I too was being observed. Roe deer are a species of the woodland edge, thriving in the margins where light meets shade, and the dynamic nature of the plant succession gives rise to an abundance of biodiversity. Their numbers have exploded over the past few decades with the absence of any natural predators to keep them in check, and they can inflict fatal damage on new saplings, but there is no denying that roe deer belong here among our woodlands. A young buck still sporting his antlers and a pair of does watch me nervously with their liquid brown eyes. They are clothed now in their winter colours; the burnished copper of their summer coats is dulled to a soft grey. Tasting the air with constantly moving lips that are framed by a white moustache, every sense is alert to potential danger.

Eventually, I can hold my awkward pose no longer and the snapping of a brittle twig beneath my foot is enough to send them scarpering. Three snow-white rumps effortlessly navigate the woodland and in three swift bounces they are gone.

* * * * *

Christmas has come early on the farm this year in the shape of three Hereford steers and an exciting avian sighting. On Christmas Eve, the lovely Helen and her excited daughter delivered our new arrivals all the way from Shropshire, where they had been bred and halter trained ready to join us here in Lincolnshire. Helen is the only breeder in the country of 'miniature' Herefords, selectively bred over the decades for smaller stature. Their eventual purpose on the farm, along with red deer, ponies, pigs and the already resident roe deer, will be to graze the land, creating a diverse mosaic of habitats which

The deer spend lot
of time alert while
grazing, looking around
then low down
... soon as they
are aware
of us
they are
likely to
flee

Young Roe
Buck

very large
eyes - beautiful
lashes

In Autumn + Winter
there are usually groups of
up to 6 deer together

shiny
nose

bright white
bottoms

They kick their
legs up lightly when
they run
with their
heads held
upright

Gross Alight!

Lots of
browns
in the
palette →

will, in turn, be able to support a greater variety of species. Low densities of grazing and browsing herbivores are crucial components of a functioning and dynamic ecosystem. The differing morphology of each type of grazer, along with their natural behaviour, fulfils a different role, each helping to shape the vegetation, their combined efforts bringing balance, complexity and diversity. As well as their impact on plants, their dung helps to fertilize the soil and distribute seeds, and the disturbance created by rootling and hooves gives an opportunity for seeds to germinate that otherwise wouldn't be able to find a foothold among the dominant vegetation.

Our choice of this native breed is largely due to their friendly nature and ease of handling. Although they are not a perfect proxy for the ancient aurochs that once grazed our islands, their specialized ruminating digestive system and broad grazing teeth will complement the delicate browsing of the deer and selective grazing of native ponies, to help increase the diversity of plants on

the farm with all of the benefits this will bring. I would love to have a fully functioning herd with all of its social complexities but given the size of the farm, for now we are grateful to start with these animals.

Paddy, Pedro and Percy have already started to settle in and exert their individual personalities. Paddy is the larger and most confident of the three. As soon as he hears the rattle of the food bucket he trundles over excitedly with Percy in close pursuit, while Pedro, by far the prettiest, his forehead a mass of tight curls, nervously waits at the rear. Despite not being remotely ready for Christmas Day and all it entails tomorrow, I can't resist the opportunity for some impromptu sketching and nip out to try and capture our new arrivals on their very first day.

Almost ready to head back inside, I scan across Lone Pasture with my binoculars and something else catches my eye. A large raptor clothed in varying shades of mid-brown, not far off the size of a buzzard, is sweeping across the field but something about it is distinctly un-buzzard like. Gliding in low circling arcs, scanning the sward for voles, it sweeps up towards Church Wood and alights on a hawthorn at the edge of the wood. The giveaway is a distinctive white band across the base of its tail. My inexpert eye identifies it as a female hen harrier, but I am later corrected by Graham, the ornithologist who surveys our farm, who could tell from my motley collection of photographs that the bird is in fact a juvenile male, likely one of this year's fledglings. Hen harriers are incredibly rare, persecution and habitat loss to blame for their dwindling numbers and I felt privileged as I watched him sweep over the farm. He continues to hunt over the farm for the next few days, disappearing during a cold snap, likely in search of milder conditions further south, but returns with the milder weather, once again browsing for voles and meadow pipits and taking refuge among the scrubby vegetation before eventually moving on. Hen harriers are ground

nesters and favour the
heather uplands for
breeding rather than our
wet lowlands, so the best I
can hope for is that he stops
by again on his winter travels,
but I add to my 'bucket list'
an ambition to catch sight of
their eccentric aerial courtship
displays one day soon and can
only hope that their tumbling sky
dance once again becomes a common sight across our skies.

The arrival of the cows on the farm marks the start of a new and exciting chapter for us. Over the next few years, as the pulse of natural regeneration that is already emerging across the land continues to strengthen and take hold, it will be robust enough to withstand low levels of grazing. We will be able to release the cows and other grazers to create disturbance, maintaining a dynamic ecosystem that can support even more species and abundance.

Our visit to Chris Jones's farm in Cornwall back in April has also triggered a cascading chain of events and with the help and support of some amazing and inspirational ecologists, we are planning to introduce a pair of beavers to Church Wood in the near future, which we expect to supercharge the development of wetland habitat across the farm.

From the moment we took the land out of cultivation, change began to happen. Slowly and imperceptibly at times, and with heated urgency at others, species have begun to appear that we'd never seen before and the overall abundance of life on the farm has surged. Over the past few years, watching the farm respond to its newfound freedom, we have begun to crystallize our vision for what the land will become. A complex system of wetlands, wood pasture, meadow and ponds, it will be rich and biodiverse. Reintroducing lost species and allowing large herbivores to keep the ecosystem active and dynamic, it will teem with life and help to ignite a recovery of nature as projects like ours catalyze more change across the country. Acting as a refuge for species clinging onto survival, we hope that our farm will inspire others in our local area who have equally unproductive land, and an interconnected vast network of wild habitats will one day streak through the farmland of Lincolnshire, complementing and supporting those who are growing food nearby.

As the land has changed, so have we. The small successes we have had so far have galvanized us and we are passionate and determined in our ambitions for the farm. The more we have learned, the more our opinions have morphed and shifted, reinforcing our convictions. At times, this has distanced us from the farming community and some of our friends who struggled to understand why we would want to turn our back on traditional farming, and perhaps who see our decision as an implicit criticism of them, despite our heartfelt protestations to the contrary. Though some still disapprove, others have come along with us, and we are eternally grateful to them for their unerring support. We have also started to become part of a different community and it has been a revelation to meet people who share our values, especially at times when we were feeling a little isolated. As the year draws to a close, I'm excited to keep things moving forward, and pushing on to make our small farm offer the most to nature that it possibly can.

Afterword

We have lost so much of our wildlife and the depressing thing is that we are barely aware of it. In my own lifetime I can remember the days of having to scrape a dense film of insect corpses from the car windscreen at height of summer, a chore that is no longer necessary. I remember as a child finding hundreds of newly minted ladybirds on my mum's plants, counting their spots and delighting in their shiny red wing cases. They are so much more scarce now. My childhood memories of going out with my dad late on a spring evening and shining a torch under the yew tree in the garden to have a peek at the hedgehogs that lived there are not something that my own children can reliably recreate. The statistics are stark and worrying. We have lost 65 per cent of flying insects in just 20 years. Seventy-three million birds have disappeared from the skies since 1970. And this is only a small fragment of the picture. The baselines against which we measure biodiversity and bioabundance were set around the 1970s when modern surveying methodologies were developed. You could be forgiven for believing that this represented an ambrosial panacea of multiplicity – a rose-tinted time when nature flourished and humans lived in harmony with wildlife in a diverse and bountiful wonderland of environmental riches. Compared with today, it probably was, but the reality is that by then we were already in deep trouble.

Every species has an impact on its environment and the other species that live within it. The interactions and the pressures that species exert on one another are part of the driving force of natural selection, moulding and shaping characteristics as biological arms races wage on every front. For much of our evolutionary history, we were just another part of this picture; a marginal species that lived and died among every other. But at some point, our increasing brain size and cognitive ability set us apart from other species. The speed with which our society and culture was then able to develop outpaced the rate at which natural selection could equip other animals with defences against our new powers. As *Homo sapiens* expanded their range, a plethora of extinctions followed. Almost every species of megafauna disappeared within an evolutionary blink of an eye once we had arrived. The remaining species of megafauna today are in Africa, our evolutionary home, where the animals had a chance to evolve a defensive response and innate fear of this deadly new species that had arrived on the scene. As millennia rolled by, we continued to strengthen our commanding control of the natural world and so intoxicated were we by our unique situation, we convinced ourselves that we had been gifted with divine privileges over the animal kingdom. We shaped gods in our own image and granted ourselves powers to decide the fates of all others. Over the past millennium, we ceased to view ourselves as part of a unified, interdependent system, and gradually we hunted and persecuted species that proved to be an inconvenience or came in to conflict with our increasingly comfortable lifestyles. We destroyed the last beavers in the 1600s and the last wolf in Scotland was slaughtered in 1680. Removing a keystone species such as a beaver or wolf can be likened to removing the ace of spades from the bottom row of a house of cards. The complex web of interactions with other species and the very fabric of the landscape is irrevocably changed once they are removed from it. The Enclosures Acts, laws enacted from the 17th to 19th centuries, took vast swathes of our countryside out of common ownership and privatized it, creating larger, enclosed farms. This resulted in habitat and biodiversity loss and accelerated the process of agricultural intensification.

The evocative poetry of John Clare paints a picture of an abundant and thriving natural world that existed before enclosure. The countryside he describes is almost mythical in its richness and diversity, and he also reminds us that, despite the monumental changes that we had already wrought, communities were still able to exist in harmony with the land, taking what they needed without dominating and destroying it.

The beginning of the Industrial Revolution, when we discovered how to unleash the energy stored within fossil fuels and lit the fuse of unfettered progress, marked the moment in time that the scales were finally tipped and we set off down a path of wanton destruction of the natural world. The decades that followed saw the industrialization of agriculture, the poisoning of our land and waterways with chemicals, and a proliferation of plastics which have polluted even the remotest and wildest parts of the Earth that still remain. We have claimed every part of the land and sea as our own.

One of the reasons for our unmitigated success as a species is our ability to adapt. A side effect of this remarkable ability is that we soon get used to a new status quo. Within just a few years we accept a reduction in birdsong and our brain tells us that it has always been that way. The effect is even greater across generations and is known as 'shifting baseline syndrome'. We simply can't feel devastated by the destruction of the world around us because we have forgotten that it was ever any different. I often hear people pooh-poohing the idea that wildlife is in trouble and citing the three sparrows on their bird feeder that morning and all the 'bloody wasps' that rudely interrupted their picnic last summer. Topics related to climate, the environment and sustainability are being taught in schools, but perhaps the stark facts that an estimated 400 species have gone extinct in the UK since 1800 or that more than half of the life in our oceans has disappeared since the 1950s, are not emphasized enough. It's often too hard for us to comprehend the extent of this loss and to imagine a world beyond the threshold of our own experiences.

Over the past few generations, we have also developed an adversarial relationship with wildlife. Plants are demonized as weeds, insects as pests and troublesome animals and birds as vermin. Over the course of writing this book, on several occasions I've had reason to tap into Google the name of particular species to fact check some aspect of their ecology. Overwhelmingly, the plethora of results that spew from the search engine are focused on how to eradicate them, from the humble field vole to the harmless wood ant. We have welcomed chemical controls into our homes and gardens with open arms. Sanitized, sterile gardens are considered desirable and we look down on those who don't comply with this cultural norm. And don't even get me started on artificial grass... Meanwhile, we are carelessly presiding over extinction after extinction, accelerating at an alarming rate.

As I write this chapter I can feel a lump starting to form in my throat. I just can't understand how people are happy to accept the loss of so much, that they are content to be handing down to their children a natural world so much more depleted and impoverished than the one that they inherited, and yet feel nothing but bile and hatred for a field of thistles or an untidy verge. Future generations of children are being robbed of wildness, of the opportunity to connect with nature, of discovering the magic of the natural world, and they have absolutely no idea. We are being given warning after warning about 'tipping points' and 'points of no return' and yet we can't seem to bring about enough change to move the needle. The impacts of climate breakdown are starting to emerge, with catastrophic droughts, apocalyptic flooding and devastating wildfires ripping through parts of the world. Sea ice is disappearing and coastal communities are beginning to understand the implications of rising sea levels. We are just starting to see that we can't exist in isolation – this wholesale destruction and elimination of nature cannot happen without the crumbling of our very foundations. Still, we don't seem to really believe it is happening. After all, this is not on our doorsteps. It's not yet our problem, let's carry on as we are. We fail to heed the warnings, shrug our shoulders, hope that someone else does something about it before it starts to affect us, and we give airtime to deniers who appeal to the fading glimmer of hope in our souls that the scientists have got it wrong.

I feel I have to mention the argument commonly raised at the mention of creating wild spaces for nature: the issue of food security. Of course we need to eat. But the biggest risk to our food security is the collapse of the natural world. We need healthy soils, abundant insect populations and clean water because these things form the foundation of farming. Even the most ardent rewilders are not arguing for taking productive land out of food production and framing the debate as food vs nature is unhelpful and distracting – the two can and must exist hand in hand.

Currently in the UK, the land use includes around 17 per cent for cereal cropping (40 per cent of which goes to feed livestock), 52 per cent for livestock grazing, 5 per cent for managed grouse moor, 2 per cent for golf courses and 0.5 per cent for growing biofuels.* The government's landscape recovery targets are aiming for 1 per cent of the UK's least productive land to be dedicated to nature. It's also worth mentioning that we waste 9.5 million tonnes of the food we produce every year at a cost of £19 billion.

It is a sign of our dysfunctional relationship with nature and our fundamental refusal to acknowledge our reliance upon it that this meagre target is so vehemently contested. Why is the media not full of blustery, spittle-flecked indignations demanding that fairways are

*Data from DEFRA.

ploughed up to provide more food for the nation? It is certain that we can't carry on as we are – life as we know it isn't sustainable without a functioning ecosystem supporting it.

Of course, we are mere individuals. It isn't in our power to make the big changes that are needed to make a difference.

And yet. If we can just learn to see the beauty in wildness. If we can learn to value the cry of a buzzard or the chirp of a grasshopper a little more highly. If we can accept an uncut lawn, or even a section of wildness beside it that hums with bees. If we can view our gardens as a shared space rather than a possession to dominate and bully into tidy submission. If we begin to see golden dandelions and architectural thistles as something precious that give life to others. If we can understand the devastating impact of spraying pesticides carelessly and change our attitudes just a little. If we change the narrative and stop referring to wildlife as pests, weeds and vermin. If we can teach our children more about the tapestry of complex interactions that exists between every species of which they are just a single thread, and show them that nature is not just 'nice to have', but is essential to their very existence.

It hasn't taken long for nature to begin returning to our farm. It hasn't taken long for us to hear a crescendo in birdsong and a proliferation in the abundance and diversity of plant life and invertebrates. We are starting to see the return of species that depend on these building blocks, and the early signs of fragile recovery. Our natural world is in such a desperate state that the merest crumb of wild space is gratefully and greedily accepted. Imagine if every household lucky enough to have some outside space allowed just a little more wildness to creep in. Imagine if we all joined together to create connected wild habitat throughout our islands. Imagine if we tolerated and learned to love more wildness in our shared spaces. Imagine what it would mean for nature and the communities that live within it. Think of how little that would cost us and what we have to gain.

Just imagine.

Acknowledgements

We owe a huge debt of gratitude to Graham Catley, who has been surveying the farm for us over the past two years. We are so lucky to be able to learn from his vast knowledge and experience. He has also been incredibly generous with his wonderful photography, which has helped to bring the project to life on our social media pages.

Thanks to Harvey Tweats and Tom Whitehurst from Celtic Rewilding for their endless enthusiasm and extensive knowledge, and to Derek Gow for helping us to bring our ideas to life. Thanks to Lincolnshire Wildlife Trust for their support, and in particular Tammy Smalley (aka Nature's pimp) and Fiona Everingham. Thank you to Chris and Janet Jones for being so generous with their time and for showing how nature-friendly farming can be done.

For helping me by reading the first draft and offering invaluable advice, thank you to Gareth Townshend, Howard and Maureen Walker, Tom Dale, Caroline Marshall, Charlotte Coulthard, Derek Gow, Harvey Tweats and Fiona Everingham.

Thanks to the team at Batsford for their support and advice, particularly Bella Skertchly, Frida Green, David Graham and Nicola Newman.

Finally, thank you to Jack for sharing this adventure with me, and letting me get totally carried away.

Index

magpie 88
mallard 47–8, 55
martin 52, 100, 133, 141, 144
mayfly 72
meadow brown 7, 79, 93, 103
meadow foxtail 82
meadow pipit 18, 64, 65, 164
meadowsweet 99
mink 115
moorhen 55–6
mosses 53, 60, 91, 159
moths 94, 106–8, 108–9, 123

nettle 108, 155, 156
noctules 109

oak 29, 42, 61, 90–3, 130, 147, 149, 159
orchid 23, 79
otter 111
owl 91, 97
    barn 7, 15, 19, 39
    little 16, 63, 157, 158
    short-eared 39–40
    tawny 11, 16, 39, 75–6, 80–1
oyster 57
oystercatcher 69, 81

painted lady
    butterfly 145
partridge 88,
peacock butterfly 103
pied wagtail 81, 139
pignut 23, 67
pioneer plants 89,

90, 145–6, 149
polecat 112, 115, 116
ponds 31–6, 55–8, 67–73, 158
pond snail 69, 119
poplar, black 61
poppy 82
privet 115

quail 75

rabbit 18, 115, 116–17, 123, 132
ragged robin 23, 67
ragwort 26, 30–1, 65, 103–4, 108
rat 98, 115
red admiral butterfly 103, 137, 156
red campion 156
redwing 10–11, 141, 147, 150
reeds 94
ringlet butterfly 93
ring ouzel 149–50
robin 16, 22, 56, 139, 141, 150
robin's pincushion 126
rushes 94, 150

St Mark's fly 64
sallow 12, 90, 97, 150
sandpiper, green 69
scrub 7, 30–1
seal 52
sedge 12
shelduck 36–7
shrike
    red-backed 29
skimmer, black-
    tailed 72

skipper butterfly 93
skylark 18, 19–21, 49, 64, 139
sloe 122
small heath butterfly 93
snipe 18, 151–2, 158–9
snowdrop 19, 22
soil health 7, 88–90, 171
sparrow 81
spider 104, 133, 137
spindle 149
squirrel 59, 91
starling 23, 26, 148
stickleback 69
stoat 37
stonechat 21
swallow 52, 64, 77–8, 80, 100, 126, 133, 140
swan 55, 69, 141–4
swift 100

tadpole 38, 69, 81, 86
teal 55
thistle 7, 10, 29, 30–1, 44, 79, 89, 103, 104, 108, 145–6, 170, 172
thrush 16, 63, 148
    mistle 81
    song 22, 139
    winter 10, 147–8
toad 32–3, 32, 38, 82, 86–8
toad spawn 33, 38, 87
trees 42–6, 90–3, 95, 109, 149, 159, 161
trefoil 82, 89, 116

trout 57

verges 30, 67, 170
vetchling 116
viper's bugloss 23, 89
vole 15, 19, 22, 39–40, 81, 115, 124, 164, 170

warbler 141
    grasshopper 61, 63, 97–8, 99
    reed 21
    sedge 63
    willow 38, 63
wasps 91, 93, 126
waterlily 82
water mint 97
water vole 115
waterways 57–8, 67–8, 111–12
wetlands 68–9, 75, 111–12, 158–9, 165
whitethroat 63, 98
willow 43, 57, 150
willowherb 65, 108, 122
wolf 168
wood anemone 56
woodcock 18, 152–4
woodland 30, 42–6, 159
woodpecker 18, 56, 109, 123
wood pigeon 117, 134
wren 11, 16, 22, 49, 59, 139

yarrow 65, 116
yellowhammer 21
Yorkshire fog 82

First published in the United Kingdom
in 2025 by
Batsford
43 Great Ormond Street
London
WC1N 3HZ

An imprint of B. T. Batsford Holdings Limited

Copyright © B. T. Batsford Ltd 2025
Text and illustrations copyright © Hannah Dale 2025

ISBN 978 1 84994 938 5

A CIP catalogue record for this book is available from
the British Library.

10 9 8 7 6 5 4 3 2 1

Reproduction by Mission Productions, Hong Kong
Printed by Toppan Leefung Printing International Ltd, China

This book can be ordered direct from the publisher at
www.batsfordbooks.com, or try your local bookshop.

Dedication

In memory of Benedict.

This book is dedicated to all trans individuals and especially to my own trans daughter whose journey has been an inspiration to me.

I hope that my writing serves to reassure and inform parents embarking on this path as well as those who want to have a better understanding of the transgender community.

Culture is often used as an excuse for discrimination. I have sought to show here that when faced with unconventional situations, the only reliable guide we have is our innate love for fellow human beings.

About the Cover Design

Yin Yang Yuan, also called Triality-One is a transgender symbol. The resemblance of the shapes within the circle to the Persian paisley or *Boteh-Jegheh*, gave me the idea for the cover design of this book.

The three elements contain symbols of Persian, Thai, and English culture as well as transgender identity.

The rose, although the national flower of England, has its origins in Central Asia and parts of the ancient Persian empire. As such, I have always loved this flower because it connects my two cultures with each other.

The church has had a strong influence both in my life and my trans daughter's life. To me, churches are a symbol of protection.

The lotus flower, marigold and jasmine are all revered in Thai Buddhism. The symbol in the middle of the Thai paisley is an interpretation of a stylised bird guardian or *chofa* that live on the peaks of each gable on the roofs of Thai temples.

The paisley is originally a Persian symbol which can be dated to the emergence of the Zoroastrian faith over three thousand years ago. In Persian art, the shape of the paisley symbolises a cypress tree bending in the wind. It is said that a cypress sapling was brought to earth from paradise by Zoroaster. There is evidence of the pattern in Persian art since at least the seventh century CE. Upright cypress trees are also depicted on stone carvings in Persepolis.

The green surrounding the Persian part of the cover design is to symbolise the cypress. The flower motif in the middle of the Persian cypress is called a 'Shah Abbasi flower,' named after Shah Abbas the Great (1571 – 1629 CE) of Iran. This motif exists in its various forms in Persian designs and particularly in carpets. Although it is named after Shah Abbas, its origins can be traced back to the Sassanid era in Iran (224 – 651 CE).

I have also incorporated a rainbow in the Persian part of the design as a nod to the LGBTQ community.

The sign at the centre of the design is the most used transgender symbol. The use of pinks and blues is also in tribute to trans colours.

Transcultural

Transcultural

Minou Bahrami

All names in this book have been changed to protect the identity of individuals described.

The only real name is that of Dr Suporn.

Of Sons and Daughters

My grandparents on my mother's side were a strange match. They had found each other through my grandmother's guardian who knew that my grandfather was looking for a wife. My grandfather was a feminist while my grandmother firmly believed that men were superior to women.

I remember talking about women's rights with my grandfather. Our religious studies teacher had told us that Islam elevated the position of women because it forbade the burial of live, new-born girls. My grandfather scoffed at this. He said, 'Iranian women do not owe Islam anything. We had two female queens ruling the empire before the Arab invasion of the seventh century. The only women Islam helped were the Arab women of the Arabian Peninsula.'

Grandmother muttered a prayer and went into the kitchen. She did not argue about these issues. She was a good Shi'a Muslim and as such had her own views about the place of women in society. My grandfather by contrast, was not religious. He believed in God but had no religion. Towards the end of her life, grandmother had taken to saying extra daily prayers to save her husband's soul. Against the wishes of her husband and her children, she had refused to learn to read and write because many years before an Imam had told her that women should remain illiterate.

My grandmother loved her sons and her grandsons more than the females in the family. We all knew this. She passed this way of thinking to my mother somehow. Or was it that my mother married a man who revived these feelings in her from the depths of her childhood?

*****

My sisters and I knew from a young age that had we been boys, both our parents would have loved us more. As well as misogynist elements in their upbringing, our parents lived under the shadow of a still born boy who had been their first child. They longed to replace him with another son but instead, they ended up with three daughters.

Preferring sons to daughters was not uncommon for my parents' generation in Iran, but the dynamic of their relationship further heightened the tensions caused by the lack of male offspring.

For my father having a son would have been an outward sign to society that he was a man capable of producing true heirs and continuing the family name. For my mother, even as a career woman, a son symbolised a protector, a man who would unconditionally stand by her side and put her difficult husband in his place.

Surprisingly, for us girls, there were some advantages attached to this situation. Our parents' preference for boys did not translate into a limitation of opportunities for us.

For one thing, we were raised in an almost gender-neutral way; perhaps because our parents were out to prove that even though we were girls, we could achieve as much as any boy.

So, all three of us grew into women who did not want to just rely on a man for our upkeep. We had ambitions and aspirations for ourselves, we all wanted to live independent lives. I never even questioned the fact that I would work to earn my own way even within a marriage.

Our mother never taught us any 'female' ways. We found our own way when it came to our outward appearance. I never wore skirts throughout my teens and had my hair cut short. I remember friends from more conservative families laughing at the way I walked too. They used to say I walked like a man. People found my walk particularly funny when I went to places where I had to wear the *chador* – the Iranian full-length veil. I was told they could see me coming a mile off even among other girls wearing the same thing.

We were also free thinkers. We were taught by both parents to question the norms of society. Given that during the course of my life, Iranian society developed many restrictive norms, imposed by the Islamic Republic, I am grateful to my parents for instilling this trait in me. Although they could have gone further when it came to their ideas about the value of sons versus daughters. There were times, however, when it would have been easier if we had been given some extra consideration at home because of our gender.

The outside world of the Islamic Republic was already heavily anti-female. My whole teenage tomboy look came from a place where I felt I could melt into the background easier and be safer if I didn't wear makeup or look feminine. My classmates were being arrested daily for trying to look feminine despite wearing the compulsory hijab. I was afraid of looking like a woman. A bit of a celebration of femininity at home would have helped me love myself more.

I was also sent abroad to study at a young age – seventeen – on my own. This was something that happened more frequently to boys in Iran. I only know of one or two other families who sent their daughters abroad at a similar age without their mothers at least. This is not to say that I think it is correct to part with teenage sons but not daughters. I know now that either gender suffers when they are so drastically separated from their family. I just think that if my family had had more traditional values, I personally could have been spared that fate.

It is also true that, most girls of my age within our social circle in Iran enjoyed the perks of being female at home. It would be considered the norm for them to spend more on clothing than boys, and of course on makeup. Most Iranian girls I knew were encouraged to dance and their beauty was celebrated and talked about within the family. They had protective fathers who cared about their safety and welfare as women. Not so with us.

Iranian boys were more frequently subjected to corporal punishment at home, but in our family our gender did not help us in this way.

One effect all of this has had on me as an adult is that even to this day, I struggle to feel feminine. Outwardly, people tell me that I am a feminine woman in the way I dress and wear makeup, but I don't feel that myself. There is a disconnect between the woman I see in the mirror and how I feel inside. Having said that, I have never doubted that I am female and heterosexual.

As a teenager, I watched my friends' more loving parents and thought about the injustice of being deprived of unconditional love just because I was a girl. I resolved to love all my future children the same, irrespective of their gender.

So it was that when I had my first child and she was a girl, I was determined that I would love her unconditionally and totally. It was me and her against the world as far as I was concerned. No one was going to make my daughter feel like she was not enough.

My Sons

After my daughter was born, there were comments from my parents. 'Your cousin who is the same age and married only one year before you, has two sons.' They were trying to pass on another layer of their disappointment in themselves on to me. This was annoying but didn't affect me in the sense that I did not feel I was letting them down. I knew how much I loved my daughter, and that knowledge sustained me.

Then, two-and-a-half years later, and thirty-two years after my parents lost their firstborn, I had a baby boy. Interestingly, I noticed a difference in my parents. They suddenly seemed more relaxed; like a spell had been broken. I was grateful that the pressure was off but at the same time felt guilty for even thinking that.

My feminist grandfather had passed away during my second pregnancy, but he had previously asked me to name the baby after him if it was a boy; so, I did that. My daughter was very protective of her little brother from the beginning. I was happy that he had an older sister. It is good for boys to have female role models.

*****

Then, when my son was six years old, I had another baby boy. There was a double rainbow in the sky the day he was born. He was a beautiful and happy child. He was so peaceful and good that at times, I felt guilty when I was alone with him. I questioned whether I was giving him more love and attention compared to my other two.

But maybe all that was meant to be. We were to know that little boy for only one year and twenty days before he died following an accident at home. The day he died will forever be the worst day of my life. That is something parents who have lost children have in common; they know which day is the worst day of their lives.

*****

Omar Khayyam (1048 – 1131 CE), Iranian poet and polymath, uses the word 'potter' to allude to God. There is a Christian hymn that reminds me of this: *'You are the potter; we are the clay; the work of Your hands…'*

This quatrain by Khayyam is ever present with me when I think of the precious child that I lost.

جامی است که عقل آفرین می زندش

صد بوسه مهر بر جبین می زندش

این کوزه گر دهر چنین جام لطیف

می سازد و باز بر زمین می زندش

There is a chalice, praised by wisdom.

One hundred kisses are bestowed upon its forehead.

The Potter of the ages creates such delicate vessels.

But then time and again, He shatters them on the ground.

*****

The older children were nine and six years old then. I reeled with pain, physical and emotional, for many months. There

14

were visits to the doctor, counsellors, and priests. I cried every day on the way to work and back in the car just so the older two children would not see me crying. I do not remember much from that time in terms of what I was doing every day.

My parents came for the funeral. They were frozen with fear and sadness. My mother cried for her own son that she had lost decades before. I comforted her. She told me to try and forget my baby. She said it was not good for me to wallow. I thought I had the right to wallow for at least a while.

*****

Now I look back, I don't know how those early days and the first few years after the baby's death affected the older children. We talked about the baby. We talked about God and Heaven and cried together but in general, I tried to present a cheery face when I was with them.

At that point, I also realised that I had imagined a whole complete future for my children. I had imagined that my younger son would be Best Man at his brother's wedding. I grieved this loss too among other things that would never be.

This loss opened emotional doors to me without any need to knock. I was suddenly a part of the huge society of parents who lose children daily all over the world. I felt that all cultural barriers were crushed, and I had access to the hearts of people in deepest Africa, China, Middle East, anywhere really. All children became infinitely more precious to me than I had ever imagined possible. When I look at any child now, I see the love that is the best measure of what it is to be human.

Another unexpected effect of losing a child was the physical pain that I lived with in the first few years. There was a pain in the depth of my stomach which was just like the pain of having been kicked repeatedly in that part of my body. At first, this pain was ever present. After the first year or so, it came and went out of the blue. Twenty-one years on, I still feel it sometimes.

The 'waves of grief' is a good analogy. In the early days, it feels as if you are standing in the ocean and being hit by unceasing, strong waves. Then, gradually, the waves become less strong and less frequent. But even years after the event, you could be minding your own business, going about your daily life and a wave can knock you sideways. That is when to others, it appears that you are crying for no reason.

*****

I also started a new, full-time job only a few months after the baby died. I had already been interviewed for the job and was expecting to start later in the year. After much deliberation, and once I realised being alone at home was too difficult for me, I started work. The job was very good for me in those first few years. It helped me survive my grief.

Within a couple of months, I was pregnant again. This was planned. I agreed with the children's father that the family should see another baby grow and live. I did not want us to be known as the family who lost a child. We were going to build a future including another child while honouring the past and the huge loss that we had all endured.

My youngest was born ten and a half months after the baby died, another boy. We were all so happy. I loved this baby for his brother too. I gave him extra kisses and cuddles for the one I had lost. The other two children were able to see him grow up and know that life doesn't have to end abruptly.

I had to take unpaid maternity leave from the new job. This was unfair but officialdom does not cater for the emotional needs of mothers who lose babies. I had to go back to work earlier than I wanted to because we could not afford losing the income. Nevertheless, I found a fantastic childminder for the new baby who I still think about and say a prayer for.

Shifting Sands

This was our family now. A daughter, nine; a son, seven; and another son, new-born. My routine was to get the baby ready in the morning and take him to work with me which was near where his childminder lived. Then I would come back and pick the older children up from after-school club. I would then make dinner and we would all eat as a family together.

By the time my youngest was two years old, cracks started showing in my relationship with the children's father.

In time there was an affair which I only found out about well over a year after it had started. I had spent that time trying to save the marriage and had suffered much humiliation. I acknowledged the pressure that the baby's death had put on the relationship. I begged and didn't beg and tried to understand, but how can anyone understand a situation that is not what it seems?

The divorce was twelve years ago but it was four years in the making. I moved house with the children. A daughter, and two sons aged seventeen, fifteen and eight when we moved house.

The older two had to navigate their teenage years with a mother who was trying to hold everything together including a full-time job. It can't have been easy. My daughter rebelled in her own way. I am glad that she did that. It is good for teenagers to let off steam especially when they have so much on at home. My older son was always easy going, present and studied hard. He spent a lot of time with his brother. All three children have always been close.

*****

So, that was then but this is now.

I now have two daughters and one son. My older son is now a transgender woman. This change has taught me much about life and love. It is the reason I am writing this essay. I hope that I can convey the richness of the beauty that comes with having a transgender child in these few pages. I hope that other parents who may find themselves in my position, will read this and be moved to see the authenticity and courage that is contained in transgender individuals.

It has not been an easy journey; least of all for my second daughter.

Within the first week of my third child's death, I had a dream. My grandmother, the non-feminist, came forward with my grandfather behind her. There was someone wrapped in a shroud sitting behind them. I could not see who it was. She said to me in Persian, 'Don't worry! We are looking after him.' I sat up in bed, bolt upright. I knew deep in my soul that I had actually seen my grandparents. The dream was a huge comfort.

Then, five years later, when I was going through the divorce, I went to see a psychic not quite knowing what they were about. This woman, who I had never seen before, stared at me, looked shocked and said, 'Your baby died! Your grandmother is here. She says 'Don't worry! We are looking after him.' I said, 'Which grandmother?' Without hesitation, she said, 'It's your mother's mother.' I cried uncontrollably. Then she said, 'Your other children will not die.' She looked concerned and emotional when she said that. I tried to shut this out of my mind. I couldn't help but feel there was something else that she was not telling me. With the passing of time, I am sure that she had seen the hardships ahead for my second daughter - Ellen.

Falling – Into Place

Ellen told me she was bisexual when she was sixteen. We were driving back from my work where she was doing her work experience for school. I didn't bat an eyelid. It was genuinely not an issue with me. I just said, 'That's fine hun. Be whatever makes you happy.' I was pleased that she felt she could confide in me of course. But I had no idea that she may have had doubts about her gender as well. At that time, she was still identifying as male.

A year later, she left me a note in my bedside table. She told me she was transgender. I did not know what this meant. I hoped that it meant she liked cross-dressing. But I looked it up and then I fell into a whirlpool of anxiety and sorrow. The thoughts going through my mind all came from a loving place. I felt sad because I had loved her body all my life. I had tended it, looked after it, worried about it getting hurt. Now, the mere idea of my child not liking her own body made me feel so sorry for her because I saw her as beautiful. I cried a lot. I shut off the idea of gender reassignment surgery because that made me afraid for her life. 'It may never get to that. Maybe she's just confused. Maybe it's just a phase. Maybe if I spend more time with her, I can get to the bottom of this and find the Real reason this is happening. Maybe she needs more male role models.' All these thoughts swam in my head as I fell further into a state of uncertainty.

Later that day, we went for a walk in the barley fields near the house. It was a sunny day. We talked and we both cried. I asked her if she felt alienated from her body and she said, 'Yes.' That sent me into deep sadness again.' I held back the panic that came from the fear of losing another child. The spectre of that operation had started to haunt me. I was holding back a lot of emotions, just trying my best to look strong and in control.

We spoke about whether she was ready to speak with her dad about this. She said, 'Not yet.' I thought that had to be her decision. Part of me also thought, 'This may all blow over before anyone else needs to know.' I was grateful for not having to cope with the fallout of other people's emotions about this just yet.

There was a therapist that I was seeing then. She asked me if Ellen had spoken with anyone except me about her feelings. I told her that I did not think so and that I felt quite lost as to how I could help Ellen. The therapist suggested counselling for Ellen so she could voice her feelings in detail to someone neutral. Ellen agreed to go. That took the pressure off me for a while. I hoped it was helping Ellen to talk but she stopped going after close to a year of therapy. Later she told me that the sessions had not been helpful.

At some stage we also went to see a psychiatrist in London. Ellen had saved her own money and paid the private consultation fee. She has always been so independent and responsible when it comes to money and her healthcare especially with regards to her transition. It was a first step, but I don't remember anything ground-breaking happening that day. I remember feeling sad when I saw her hand the fee to the doctor. This was money that she could have spent on going out with her friends like a lot of young people do. This was my first glance at how seriously she felt about her transition.

On those early days, when I saw trans women in town, I used to worry about how Ellen would be treated when she was fully out. Transphobia put the fear of God into me. Ellen was such a gentle person. She still is. She is also hilariously witty, laid back and kind. The thought of anyone being aggressive towards her for being true to herself angered me and made me afraid.

Ellen finally told her father one year after she had left me the note. I agreed to meet him to discuss 'the situation.' It was an awkward meeting. It is fair to say that we were both in a state of denial. While Ellen was growing up, she had not shown any interest in typically female activities or things. She had not put on mine or her sister's clothes or played with dolls. Thomas the Tank Engine and Bob the Builder were her firm favourites. But she was not a rough and tumble kind of boy either. She used to play football but in a very disengaged, half-walking, half-running kind of way. Once when I asked her why she wanted to play, she said, 'I like spending time with my friends.'

This was my first and last talk with Ellen's father about her transition. After that meeting, I decided to carry on biding my time. I was going to be in that zone of total acceptance for whatever Ellen decided to do. She did exceptionally well in her A-levels and was accepted in the university of her choice to read Computer Science.

In the meantime, there was the question of the gap year. She had some money saved that would allow her enough funds to go travelling to some distant places. I suggested some friends and family in the US. Her first destination was Hawaii then Texas then San Francisco. The people she was staying with were very different to adults that she had known in Britain. I thought it was good for her to see alternative lifestyles. Part of me thought maybe if she saw people who were happy living less conservative lives, this would provide her with a middle ground that she had not considered – something between being trans and totally conventional or heterosexual. No matter how hard I tried, my fear of the operation would not go away.

The fact that escaped me at the time was that being trans was not an idea that had occurred to Ellen while searching for an alternative identity. That is just who she was. She could no more decide to be just a bit hippy or gay instead of trans than I could. I should also say that my biggest fear for her was transphobia and the fear of permanent harm due to the Gender Reassignment (GR) surgery. I now know that much of this fear was due to the loss of my third child.

At no point did I think that Ellen should not be trans because I did not like trans individuals. My only concern was for her welfare and physical safety.

Nevertheless, the gap year went by, she came home and went off to university. Still using her male name. At that point, the only outward sign of femininity was her long hair – which is not necessarily a feminine marker anyway.

Once at university, Ellen started taking hormones. Her appearance began to change. We all started the process thinking of her as female. She didn't talk to me about the details of her life, but I always reminded her that I was there if she wanted to talk. Then she also changed her name. She asked me for an alternative Persian name which I provided.

We started using feminine pronouns when we talked about Ellen. This was difficult to start with. It particularly annoyed me because pronouns don't have any gender in Persian. Every time I said, 'he,' I got annoyed with the English language for putting me in this position.

A strange change was coming over me at this point. I could see that I was slowly losing the son I had known for eighteen years. My son was becoming my daughter, but I had all the memories of the little boy and the young teenager that I had loved. My grandfather's name was gone too. The old idea of the boys being each other's Best Man was completely dashed.

It was through talking to my youngest that I began to realise that there was some legitimate grief present for us as Ellen's family.

We were on a train together, coming back from London where we had gone to see the oldest two. My youngest was then only about twelve years old. He had tears in his eyes. He said he was sad because he did not have a brother anymore. I said that Ellen was the same person only she looked a bit different on the outside. 'We haven't lost the other person; we have gained a new version of them.' Even as I said these words, I realised that I had not dealt with this loss myself because I had been so busy trying to deal with my various anxieties about Ellen's safety.

Navigating the Persian 'Gulf'

The idea of losing a son and gaining a daughter reminded me of that other aspect of having a trans woman as a child: my parents' obsession with male heirs. The fact that Ellen had been the first male child in the family since they lost their firstborn and that she had carried my grandfather's name, had a certain significance for them.

I decided all that had to go on the back burner. My parents didn't visit often. They were also not close to the children. I spoke with Ellen about this. I explained that I thought the grandparents did not need to know yet because we needed to find our own footing before we could deal with other people's reactions. I guess what I was saying was that 'I' needed some more time because I would have been the person in the firing line, and I did not have the mental energy to cope with my parents' emotions at the time.

Had Ellen been a trans man, my own feelings about losing a daughter and gaining a son would have been the same. It would have been a change including a feeling of loss and a feeling of gain. I did not give a toss about which gender had changed but somehow, I thought that my parents may feel differently. I did not want to engage in conversations about issues that were irrelevant to me but highly agitating and upsetting for them. I felt both parties should be spared this exchange for the time being.

My decision also came from a place of compassion for my parents. The death of my baby had been a shock for both. The divorce caused them great shame in their social circles in Iran. They had thought the world of their son-in-law and had sung his praises to all their relatives and friends. I still remember my father's words, 'But he said in his wedding speech that we hadn't lost a daughter, rather we had gained a son.' Those words had meant so much to my father who had wanted a son all his life.

They both aged visibly after the divorce. My mother's depression became almost debilitating. When we spoke on the phone, her only conversation was about how awful my father was. I could not confide in her or expect her to take on yet another concern.

It was too much to ask of them, now in their seventies, to understand Ellen's transition. They would have treated the issue as another huge loss reinforced by their own attitudes to gender.

*****

My father was very proud of his family heritage. He came from a village in the deepest South of Iran – the village has now expanded into a small town. My father's maternal grandfather was the Sheriff in the village. He was in charge of fifty armed horsemen and kept the peace. By all accounts he was a chivalrous man.

The concept of chivalry is strong in Persian culture. Some research has even shown that this concept may have found its way to Europe through ancient Persia.

Persian speakers are familiar with the word *javānmard*. It literally means 'young man' but when you use that word, everyone understands the meaning as 'chivalrous.' The word for 'man' in Persian is *mard*. In Turkish this same word is a proper name for boys – written as Mert. The word itself carries a lot of meaning. When you describe someone as *mard*, you could at the same time be saying that they are a 'real man.' Again, the concept of chivalry comes into this. A *mard* is someone who will fight for the honour of the womenfolk and his family. He looks after the poor and the destitute. He is physically and mentally strong. He can be relied upon under all circumstances.

By contrast, the word *nāmard* is an insult of the highest order. It means something like 'unman.' If you describe someone as *nāmard*, you are saying that they are useless in all the ways that a *mard* is celebrated.

Maybe I was being too anxious, but I could not have all these words and concepts and references to the real men in the family unleashed on me. I did not even want to imagine the angry words I ran the risk of hearing; words that perhaps could not be unheard.

To be fairer to my parents, I simply did not have the headspace to cope with their almost certain troubled reaction. I felt I needed all the mental energy I could muster for Ellen.

The Politics of Deceit

As well as the purely cultural concerns I had, Iranian politics added an extra layer of intolerance to my family's attitude towards the LGBTQ community.

My family never had any sympathy with the Islamic Republic, but the fact of living under such an oppressive regime, can have a negative influence on some people without them realising.

Sadly, but predictably, unhealthy cultural norms in Iran can also reinforce the discriminatory laws of the Islamic Republic at times. At a purely cultural level, Iranians of my parents' generation are generally not open minded about the LGBTQ community in Iran. When early on the Islamic Republic made homosexuality illegal and punishable by death, there was no widespread objection to this ruling.

The first instance of this execution ruling that I remember is a story I heard from a friend who was imprisoned for her political beliefs when she was still a teenager. She told us the story of the gay men who were paraded through the women's wing of the prison on the way to their execution. The women were ordered under threat of torture to shout insults at them and spit at them as they went past.

As executions increased, the gay community who were already not so visible, were driven underground. Sympathetic parents with LGBT children panicked for their children's safety and encouraged them to hide their true self in order to save their lives. On the other hand, among traditional, conservative families a gay child became even more of a disgrace because of the execution sentence that reinforced the idea of homosexuality as an immoral trait.

In my own family, people pretended that no one was gay even though we had a few gay relatives. My parents' decision was not to talk about it. This could have been as much due to a desire to protect that individual from death as to anything else.

In 1987, Ayatollah Khomeini, issued a Fatwa saying that Gender Reassignment (GR) surgery was *Halal* – permitted. On the face of it, this was a broadminded ruling. But at the heart of this Fatwa lay the sinister workings of Khomeini's mind. The ruling clergy in Iran are masters of deception. This fatwa is a prime example. It appears to be tolerant of transgender individuals, but it is in fact a destructive anti-gay measure with debateable outcomes for the trans population in Iran.

As a result of this Fatwa, Iran is second only to Thailand in the world in terms of the number of Gender Reassignment (GR) surgeries performed.

The Islamic Republic believes there are no such people as Iranian homosexuals – in fact, in 2010, the President of the Islamic Republic said as much publicly. Consequently, it is argued that any man who wants to sleep with men, must really be female and in need of GR surgery. The same applies to lesbians.

I have personally heard the stories of at least two homosexual individuals who have had the surgery and then committed suicide afterwards.

Life is not easy for those who are genuinely transgender either. Whether before or after the operation, they are still treated as outcasts and cannot find employment. Most leave their families or hometowns, ending up in Tehran homeless and jobless. This road often leads to prostitution as they struggle to feed and house themselves.

I remember walking in Tehran with an elderly aunt the last time I was there for my mother's funeral. At that point, Ellen had only just started her journey of transition. My aunt casually said that there were transgender women soliciting on that street. I was not ready for what I saw. In the Islamic Republic, these trans women were unveiled and in full make up. I admired their brazenness. One of them was whispering something to a soldier in a doorway. I felt very afraid for her.

The sad fact here was if you mentioned 'transgender' to my aunt, this had been her only encounter with trans individuals. The government had marginalised the trans community and had thus reinforced harmful stereo types of them. It was a vicious circle. I thought of one day maybe having to debunk all this for my parents. It seemed like an impossible task at the time.

*****

That encounter also flooded my mind with questions about the issue of hijab. We were told at school that we had to cover our hair because women's hair emanates special rays that blind men with desire and cause them to sin. We were told we had to cover our hair to protect men from committing sins. So, if these trans women were born boys, would their hair never have that quality? Or does something happen if you take hormones whereby your hair becomes a device for sin? The science of it was ridiculous, not to mention non-existent.

In fact, so much of the issue of compulsory hijab is about stripping women of individual ways of expressing themselves.

It is a means of control. The bigots who support the Islamic Republic, do nothing but judge and discriminate against anyone who shows any trace of individuality. This treatment has spread to other sections of society including the LGBTQ community. Sadly, the negative portrayal of this community by the Islamic Republic has had a detrimental effect on the way they are perceived in Iranian society.

The irony is that the officials who pass judgement on the trans community and limit their opportunities, driving them to a life in the Iranian underworld, are themselves corrupt and full of duplicity while the trans community are just trying to be their true self and survive.

In another quatrain, the great Omar Khayyam says,

شیخی به زنی فاحشه گفتا مستی

هرلحظه به دام دگری پا بستی

گفتا شیخا هر آنچه گویی هستم

اما تو چنانکه می نمایی هستی؟

A holy man said to a prostitute, 'You are drunk.'

'You ensnare yourself in a different trap with every moment that passes.'

The woman said, 'O! Man of God, I am whatever you say.'

'But are you what you seem to be?'

A Need-to-Know Basis

All this intolerance was so far removed from the culture that Ellen had grown up in that I felt I had to protect her from the knowledge of these attitudes. My final decision was that I will only tell my parents if I must. Possibly if either of them travelled to Britain to visit or if we had to meet up for a family gathering elsewhere.

My mother passed away without ever knowing that Ellen was transgender. My father is still alive, but he suffered a stroke during the Covid-19 pandemic which has left him unable to speak. Travel to Britain is impossible for him because of the state of his health and strict British visa regulations. So, he still doesn't know about Ellen being transgender.

This is not a perfect situation, I know. But at this point, I don't even know how much my father can understand of what I tell him. He has many issues of his own to deal with including his health and being in Iran on his own without his three children. He has a full-time carer, who is a young man. I hope that in his old age, he takes comfort in having a constant male companion. Maybe in his state of confusion, he even feels he is with the son he never had. I feel that my father's health could be impaired if the peace and stability that he has finally achieved after his stroke, is disturbed.

If you have seen the film Everything, Everywhere, All at Once (2022), you may notice some common themes between my life and that of the Chinese American family with the gay daughter. If I had been put into a situation whereby Ellen had to see her grandparents again, of course, I would have explained everything to my parents. But I doubt that situation will ever arise.

It must also be said that it is not the case that all Iranian grandparents harbour prejudice against a transgender grandchild. Among my aunts and uncles, a few of them do know about Ellen and they are completely accepting. Sometimes I think another reason I could not be open with my own parents was that I was not sure of their love. Having felt the adverse effects of feeling unloved, I did not want to expose Ellen to the same fate.

What I am certain of is that shame was not the reason for keeping my parents in the dark. I have always been proud of all my children for the good people that they are.

The Road to Enlightenment

Ellen's transition journey took ten years. After formally changing her name and starting on hormones, she had a couple of relationships with Queer individuals and developed her own sense of style which included having a few tattoos and wearing a lot of black. She did well at university and immediately after graduation found a good job in London.

I was still worried for her, but all the outward signs were that she was on her chosen path and doing well. For me it was as if we were driving on two parallel roads. I occasionally glanced over at her road to see that she was OK.

*****

What I could not do was understand her need to be a different gender. That is something I could not do any more than make myself fancy women. I had to accept that there is no point in analysing the reasons for this need in Ellen. Some friends spoke of Ellen's lack of male role models. Someone said, 'He identifies with you, that's what's happened. A good psychiatrist can sort this out.' But I refused to go there. This was Ellen's life.

Something my eldest daughter said to me early on, had stayed with me. Once when I was worried about Ellen's future and safety, her sister said, 'Mum, this isn't about you, it's about Ellen.' It was a bitter pill to swallow but I saw the wisdom in those words. Me trying to find reasons for why Ellen had these feelings about her body was not going to help anyone. I was not likely to find an answer either. She was transgender. That was that. There doesn't have to be a reason. Just like I don't look for reasons why I am a cis woman

– that is, a woman whose gender identity aligns with the sex she was assigned at birth.

Nevertheless, I still fell into asking, 'Why?' from time to time. The root of this was again fear. In my toughest moments, I used to plunge into panic imagining that Ellen had had the operation but regretted the outcome.

Some of my well-meaning friends were part of this problem. People would come to me having heard the latest worst-case scenarios of operations gone wrong or individuals who had tried to reverse the surgery and failed.

I guess they were trying to warn me of dangers in case I could do something about halting Ellen's transition before it was too late. One person sent me the complete video of a GR surgery which I never watched. Another invited me to a dinner party with a trans woman present who had had GR surgery but was still unhappy.

In time I learnt to tell these people to just respect Ellen's wishes like I have and to stop trying to educate me about the process. I just said, 'I'm taking my cue from Ellen. She will tell me whatever I need to know.'

Other friends were by contrast almost in denial that this should be an issue for me. One woman laughed when I told her Ellen was transgender. She said, 'So your boy wants to be a girl!? Ha ha!' I immediately said to her to stop and consider how she would feel if her son was in the same position. Her facial expression changed immediately. She suddenly looked sad.

Another reaction was, 'How lovely! I am surprised at you that you are at all worried. That is a discriminatory attitude you know. You should celebrate that your daughter feels secure enough to confide in you. I'm disappointed.' This woman has a son herself, but she had not even stopped to think about the physical risks involved both in terms of the surgery and transphobia. When I pointed this out to her, she too went quiet.

My medical friends could also be dismissive. One of them said, 'It's not a vital organ. Her life wouldn't be in danger.' But again, what about the emotional risks? Any surgery is a risk. Any parent would be worried even if their child was having an appendix removed.

One time I was having a party and had invited someone who did not know that Ellen was transitioning, but they had known her as a boy. I asked that person's friend to let him know before they arrived. I did not want Ellen to have to face any uncomfortable glances or questions. The guy in question was a lovely person, but I just wanted to be sure that he knew about Ellen before he arrived so that he wouldn't inadvertently blurt anything out. I had seen him do a similar thing before.

Another guest who was there early, heard me on the phone. She started shouting at me about why I should feel I had to explain Ellen to anyone. She did not understand that I was trying to protect my child. She did not have children herself. Maybe that was the reason.

Many people tended to be two dimensional about the issue. It was generally either, 'No problem at all' or 'Let's panic!' Naturally, I gravitated towards those who occupied a middle ground, who listened and understood. My philosophy was one of 'live and let live.' So, people who interfered too much in my life were put aside over time.

My attitude eventually settled into, 'I don't know anything about what it feels to be trans. I can't presume to know what Ellen should do with her body. She is the only person who knows what her needs are. It is up to her to tell me what she wants to do. It is not up to me to tell her what she should do.'

No one had the moral upper hand here. Ellen is honest and kind. She had to be free to choose the life she wanted no matter what society's judgement or my concerns for her safety dictated.

Hafez of Shiraz (1315 – 1390 CE) sums this up nicely. Scoundrel is a word he uses to mean people that sanctimonious religion disapproves of.

عیب رندان مکن ای زاهد پاکیزه سرشت

که گناه دگران بر تو نخواهند نوشت

من اگر خوبم اگر بد، تو برو خود را باش

هر کسی آن درود عاقبت کار که کشت

O! Pious man! Do not find fault in 'scoundrels,'

For you shall not be accountable for the sins of others.

Whether I am good or bad, you go and tend to yourself.

In the end, everyone will reap what they have sown.

*****

So, Ellen and I went on not really talking about her thoughts. In time, I started believing that she was not interested in the GR surgery. I had heard that some trans people never have this. This calmed me down a little and I got used to the way things were, thinking that Ellen had made her decision about not having the operation.

In the build up to the Covid-19 pandemic however, Ellen resigned from her job. There were issues with her manager who was not giving her enough space for creativity. After her resignation, she seemed to have lost her confidence in finding another job in the same field. She remained in the same high rent flat in London but started doing lesser paid jobs. Then I became really concerned for her well-being.

At around the same time however, when the pandemic started in earnest, because her new job was in the hospitality industry, she could not work and was put on furlough. We spoke on the phone and decided that if she vacated her room in the shared flat, she could come back home while the pandemic lasted. This situation was a blessing for both of us.

I got to have my daughter at home where I knew she was safe. Ellen got to be in a safe space and was able to gather her thoughts and apply for jobs relevant to her qualifications as a software engineer. She did find work with a company in London and was initially able to work from home until the pandemic finished and she was able to find a flat and move back to London.

A significant event that happened while Ellen was staying with me during the pandemic was that she started taking online confirmation instructions to be accepted in the

Catholic church. Ellen had attended a Catholic primary school, but in her teenage years, she lost interest in God and religion. There was never any pressure on her from me to go back to church. She just found her own way back.

Ellen went to a Dominican friar for her instructions. The friars did not pass any judgements. They knew her story and were completely accepting. I felt comforted by this turn of events. It was good to think that Ellen could belong to a church once she left home again and went back to London. I also thought she could pray and have a spiritual anchor if times got rough. The day she was accepted into the church was a happy day.

All this time, we talked about her saving her money thinking this would come in handy once she had to pay a deposit for her next London accommodation.

As it was, she did save money but kept it for her operation that she was now planning to have. I did not know about this until a few months after she had moved out. I went to see her in London, and we talked about it. I shed a few tears. It was both a shock and a relief. I had not expected the news and had been living with a different future in my head. That was the shock part. The relief was because I saw in Ellen's words and in her eyes that she really wanted this. She had considered all risks and costs and after ten years had no doubt that this was what she wanted to do.

She said there was a clinic in Thailand that she wanted to go to. This was because of the clinic's reputation and experience. I said, 'I will come with you for however long it takes.'

*****

When I got home, I cried again. I was afraid of what could happen in Thailand, but I knew with every fibre of my being that I had to be there. I phoned a dear aunt, and we cried a little together. She said, 'You must go. You have made the right decision, but God give you strength.'

The Land of Golden Buddhas

The Buddha (563 – 483 BCE) is alleged to have achieved enlightenment under a Bodhi Tree in Bodh Gaya, India. As I embarked on my journey to Thailand, knowing very little about this deeply religious, Buddhist country, I had no idea that the industrial town I was heading for was going to be the place where I found complete peace with Ellen's decision. Chon Buri was to be my place of enlightenment – so far as a complete understanding of my transgender child was concerned.

*****

We booked our plane tickets six months before the flight. But before I knew it, I was in Heathrow waiting to meet up with Ellen and her friend Sally who was also going to have GR surgery. They had face masks on and explained that the operation could not go ahead if they contracted Corona. It was a comfort for me to see Ellen with her friend, two people going through the same journey, supporting each other just by being together.

Ellen and I had a look round the duty-free shops. I bought her a pretty notebook so she could keep a journal. I thought the journal would come in handy in the hospital while she was going to be quite immobile. She was due to stay in the hospital for a week including the five-hour operation. I had armed myself with a Sudoku book, a crossword book and some erasable pens, a book of short stories and my embroidery.

I had seen pictures of a lovely swimming pool on the hotel website. So, I packed swimming stuff and sun lotion and summer dresses, sandals, and a pair of trainers. On Ellen's advice, I also packed a travel washing line and some handwashing liquid for clothes. My total luggage was fourteen kilograms.

This was a real step into the unknown. I had no idea at all what to expect. I had no knowledge of the details of the operation or the aftercare apart from the basic information that Ellen had given me. Ellen had also said that the hotel was linked to the hospital, so all GR surgery patients stayed in the same hotel.

I imagined that we would meet some interesting trans women, a few of them hopefully accompanied by their mothers. I hoped to make friends with some of the other mums. We had a bond already, even though I had not yet met any of them.

The eleven-hour flight went by quicker than I expected. Sudoku and in-flight movies helped. The first thing we did after going through border control and picking up our suitcases was to get a SIM card for our phones. Then we went out to the main hall of the airport where a young Thai woman was waiting for us with a sign. So far, what I noticed about Thailand was that women were very visible as airport employees. Some of them were doing quite physical work as well, wearing uniform appropriate for the weather. I thought of women in Iran and how they suffer in hot weather with compulsory hijab. It was thirty degrees outside.

The drive to the hotel took around one hour. The car was comfortable and air conditioned. We were given bottles of cold water. The woman who had picked us up was merrily chatting to the male driver. The scenery was quite industrial with glimpses of the odd very large and golden temple complex here and there.

When we arrived at the hotel, the first thing I noticed was a mini temple outside the entrance to the lobby. There were dolls in the temple in various poses. Some were sitting down, some standing, some dancing. There were offerings of soft drinks and marigolds for the occupants of the temple. The dolls represented the spirits of people who had lived in that location before. I later saw many of these structures in Thailand. I reflected on how I would have loved seeing something like this every day as a little girl.

We checked into our room on the fifth floor. I looked around at this place which was going to be our home for the next few weeks. It felt safe.

Of Mothers and Sisters

Starting on our first morning, we met trans women from all over the world at breakfast. At first, we saw Rebecca from the US. Then there was Emilie from Norway, Danya from Israel, Hilary from Australia, and the list went on.

This is when I started feeling a sense of peace wash over me. All the trans women who were there seemed happy. Some were pre-op like Ellen and were looking forward to having the operation with some apprehension. Others were post-op and happy with the outcome and the aftercare. They were all such gentle people too.

There was a real sense of sisterhood among them. It was more than witnessing a get together of women. These were women who understood each other's pain and each other's journey through life.

*****

I finally fully understood, on our first evening together in the hotel restaurant, that being trans was such an indisputable part of these women, that having this operation made them feel liberated at last. It was the last step for them to being their authentic self.

Until then, although I had reassured myself regularly that Ellen was absolutely sure about her decision, I had not understood the force of nature that drives the feelings of trans women. I was humbled by their courage and their authenticity. They were taking physical risks to become a woman, not to mention the huge financial commitment they had undertaken to be there.

So, there I was, a middle-aged heterosexual cis woman in the company of younger, mostly professional trans women who had made sacrifices to be something that I had done nothing to earn, but society did not object to me calling myself 'woman,' and yet, there were debates going on in the UK about whether trans women were 'real' women or not. To me, they deserved the label 'woman' just as much as I did.

Throughout the trip, I found the company of trans women engaging and stimulating. Granted, they were from a certain section of the population in their respective countries.

They had all been able to save the money for the operation – in total, including hotel and air fare costs, this was around twenty thousand pounds - and to take enough leave to come and stay in Thailand for at least one month. So, a certain level of education among them was to be expected. Interestingly at least fifty percent of them were software engineers. They joked about this themselves. I said, 'There must be a PhD for someone in there somewhere.'

We had a few hilarious nights talking about the potentially embarrassing situations they had to deal with during their various medical appointments. There were one or two very funny individuals who were frank about all aspects of their treatment. They could have honestly been successful stand-up comics.

*****

One pre-surgery day that has stayed with me is when a group of us went to the main shopping mall in Chon Buri. We were all using an app called 'grab,' which could be used for calling taxis, moped rides or ordering food amongst other things.

Amy and Gabrielle, a truly sweet couple from Texas said they would show us around. Gabrielle was a cis woman and had come to Thailand to support Amy in the surgery. That surgery was now completed. The couple were making a last trip to the mall to buy presents for people back home, mainly people who had looked after their animals while they were away. I briefly thought of my lovely American neighbour and my English partner back home, looking after the house and the cat.

We went in two cars. What struck me the whole time we were out was how much everyone was looking out for everyone else. The post-op patients had these cushions which are like triangular donuts for sitting on. This reminded me of a similar cushion I was given after my first baby was born. I still remember the discomfort.

We were shown where to buy food and toiletries. Some of the girls bought phones. Ellen bought a couple of comfortable dresses. On the way back, Gabrielle told us to ask any questions we could think of. Everyone was so keen to help.

*****

During our last pre-op breakfast at the hotel, I met Anita, an Israeli mum who was there with her daughter. We both looked at each other when she said she was from Israel, and I said I was British-Iranian. Then we quickly agreed that both Iran and Israel were run by people we did not respect. I spoke of what a shame it was that so many Jewish Iranians had left the country since the revolution of 1979. Anita said, 'Oh? Would you like them to come back?' I said, 'Of course. Iran is their home. They had lived there for three thousand years since the time of Cyrus the Great until the mullas took over.'

47

Anita was the first mother I met on the trip. I felt a feeling of closeness to this Israeli woman as soon as I set eyes on her.

Shared Anticipation

The surgery was usually at 08:30 and the patient was admitted the day before. Admission to hospital took place at noon on the day before the surgery. I went to the hospital with Ellen. She had her own private ensuite room with a fridge, microwave and tea and coffee making facilities. There was a camp bed for me to sleep on and a comfortable bed that someone else could easily sleep on as well.

Every patient had the picture of a Disney princess on the door. I think this was mainly because hospital staff found all these foreign names hard to pronounce or remember, so the princess names became kind of pseudonyms. Ellen's princess was Jasmine which made us both smile. I wondered if they had done that on purpose. It seemed too much of a coincidence for them to have chosen the only Middle Eastern princess for Ellen.

There were a couple of restaurants in the hospital concourse and a very nice French bakery. But that first night, Ellen had some of the hospital food and I had a pot noodle from the 7-Eleven supermarket in the concourse. This was another surprise for me in Thailand. There are so many 7-Elevens on every street.

*****

Ellen and I did not talk about the risks attached to the operation before she was admitted. She had looked into it and did not want to dwell on all the things that could go wrong. I respected her decision. There is a quote that says, 'Worry makes you suffer twice.' I firmly believe in this approach.

49

Before we fell asleep, we talked of how life-changing the outcome would be. I slept on the camp bed.

In the morning, the nurses rushed in and were so quick to take Ellen away that I almost missed saying goodbye to her.

Then I had at least a five-hour wait, so I went back to the hotel. My new Israeli friend Anita had suggested coming with me to the local area around the hotel to show me where all the useful shops were. So, we met up and walked off in the streets of Chon Buri. I knew she was trying to keep my mind off what was happening in the hospital. Her company was much appreciated.

It is fair to say that the town is not a beautiful place. But I had already developed a true liking for the people of Chon Buri. The staff at the clinic and the hospital were so kind, polite and even-tempered. The hotel staff were the same. The whole atmosphere of the hotel with so many kindred spirits around, was comforting and safe. I do miss that place.

Anita and I went to the nearest large supermarket where I bought more washing powder, washing up liquid, sponge, and various snacks. She pointed out some bolster cushions and said they would be useful and a tray table with short, foldable legs for eating in bed. We stopped to say hello to a woman who had a small clothing alterations shop. She just had a sewing machine on the pavement. Anita said she had taken her daughter's skirt there once.

*****

On our way back, we met a monk in his saffron robe who spoke good English. He said he had visited Manchester a few years back. He told me which taxi to get for the beach and then walked off towards the temple that was next to the hotel. Anita and I said goodbye quickly as I wanted to swim, have lunch and then go to hospital.

Anita was travelling back to Israel the next day. While we chatted, we swapped stories about how we had found out that our daughters were trans. We were both single mothers. Anita was a language teacher too. She taught Hebrew to Jewish Ethiopian children. Even as I write these words, I feel a true affinity with that woman. We understood each other's lives. We were also similar people in the way we had dealt with the course our daughters' lives had taken.

Anita later came to the hospital to see Ellen after her surgery, but I didn't see her again before she left because I had to be in hospital with Ellen. She had left me a present with one of the girls. It was a hand crocheted, white jellyfish in a transparent box. I remembered that she told me she loved boxes when we were in the supermarket.

*****

Emilie from Norway, a softly spoken trans woman whom I had first met on our trip to the shopping mall, offered to come to the hospital with me and Anita when we were going to see Ellen post-op on the day of the surgery. Again, the camaraderie was so heart-warming. We talked in the 'grab' taxi about what this operation meant to trans women. I said I would be so happy just to see Ellen swim again. She had not been swimming since she came out as trans but as a child, she had been a real water baby. I remembered throwing her in the water when she was a toddler, and she would always come up laughing. She was later a very good swimmer too.

Then Emilie said that she had not been able to swim for a year or so after she came out as trans because their pool would not let her use women's changing rooms. Eventually she had come up with the idea herself that she could use the changing room for the disabled. This year of not being able to swim had been painful for her because it meant that she could not take her little boy swimming.

*****

When we arrived at the hospital, I went to the nurses' station on the ward and was told that Ellen was in her room already. Everything had happened quicker than expected. The nurses said that the surgery had gone very well, and that Ellen was fine. I felt a weight lift off my shoulders. Emilie and Anita stood at the door just to make sure we were ok and then went to visit other people on the ward. Emilie was also a software engineer. She had come over on her own, as had about thirty percent of the patients. Her recovery was rather quick, and she was going back soon. I am glad I got the chance to get to know her a little even though we may never meet again.

I have an almost physical memory of the support that I felt around me on the day of Ellen's operation. My new friends were looking out for me while I was almost sleepwalking through the day. I do not know how I would have coped without anyone to share the day with.

That Singular Surgeon

The days in the hospital merged into one. We had to be up early as the surgeon visited at eight O'clock every morning. Once I slept through and as the medics marched in, I sat up on the camp bed wearing my Thai pyjamas with my hair looking ridiculous. The surgeon looked at me compassionately. He was a kind man. I knew this from the tales of his interactions with the girls.

They all spoke fondly of him and said that he was a serious man but caring and professional. He had recently started training a female colleague and she was beginning to operate under his supervision as well.

The clinic had started out twenty years before by a Dr W Suporn who had now retired and passed his mantle on to these two younger surgeons.

During my chats with the trans women in the hotel I learnt more about the female anatomy than I had ever done. I gathered from what the post-op patients told me that the procedure used by this clinic was a specific method developed by Dr Suporn which exactly replicated a vagina with all its sexual functions and sensitivity in a cis woman. This was powerfully reassuring for me but also mind blowing.

A German patient, a software engineer who liked laying out the details of such things, explained that every single part of the female sexual organ is replicated using tissue already available in the body. Parts of the body were re-used and stitched so that post surgery, the patient had a fully functioning vagina.

*****

53

One night, in the hotel restaurant, when I came across the poem at the beginning of this book, I felt it was written for Dr Suporn and his surgeons. I read it for the girls in the hotel. We were all so moved by it.

The poet is Parvin E'tesami. She is Iran's first female poet of the twentieth century. Her father took great pride in educating her. As the poem shows, she was a feminist and an impressive woman for her time. During her brief marriage, she must have understood the gender gulf between herself and her conservative husband. She did not stay in the marriage long, returning to her father's house after a few months. When she died of typhoid in 1941, she was only thirty-four years old.

It is conceivable that she would have met the surgeon she describes in the poem. From what the girls in the hotel were saying, the first GR operations were carried out in the years between the two world wars in Berlin. It could also be that Parvin never saw this surgeon but heard about him and recorded a fictitious conversation. Her style of poetry often consists of dialogues.

The poem should not be taken at face value. I personally do not see it as an anti-man poem but rather a pro-trans one. Parvin is saying that there is nothing wrong with a man becoming a woman and in fact this could be a force for good. Indeed, from what I have seen of trans women, they seem to embody the best of both sexes. They are gentle but strong, fragile but courageous. Not that either of these adjectives are male or female, but in my experience these seemingly contradictory attributes combine in trans women in a safe, reassuring way.

I find perceptions of trans women being a threat to others to be utterly misplaced. To me, they represent a creative and gentle force which is in short supply in our world today.

In time, I began to see the surgeons who performed these operations as saviours. Without exception, all the women I met at the hospital and the hotel, blossomed after the surgery. They were tired and at times in pain but carried serene smiles on their faces. It was a healing experience to be around them.

One account of a pre-op appointment with the surgeon will always stay with me as one of the funniest encounters I have ever heard.

Surgeon, 'Would like to have a *large* vagina?'

Patient, 'No! Of course, I wouldn't like a *large* vagina! Who would want a *large* vagina?'

Surgeon – still serious, 'OK then, let's say, a *deep* vagina. Would you like a *deep* vagina?'

Patient, 'What do you mean by *deep*?'

Surgeon, 'six to eight inches.'

Patient – using the first finger on each hand to indicate a distance, 'My boyfriend is about this big, I guess. How many inches is that?'

Surgeon – still serious, 'Yes, that would be a *deep* vagina.'

A Child Reborn

I can now say that I was in a state of disbelief when I saw Ellen after the operation. She looked the same of course. I was trying not to think of her injuries. She was weak and exhausted. She was also on morphine and pain killers and antibiotics amongst other things. I was surprised that she seemed to follow what I said. We had a short conversation. She said she was ok. She was happy. That was the best part of the outcome. We both cried with happiness and relief. Just a few tears but it was enough for me to know that I had now understood her journey. I was at peace with her decision and proud of her for knowing her own mind and staying true to herself.

It was a strange feeling to have a new daughter without having given birth to one. Although I had accepted Ellen as female before the operation, this was different. I think it was the same for her. She was now a woman; a woman who could not give birth, but there were so many female-born women in the world who could not bear children. As far as we were concerned, her gender was unquestionably female now.

There were a lot of comparisons to be made with childbirth. Ellen and I talked about the risks involved with the GR surgery and they were not dissimilar to postpartum issues with various tears inside the body. The aftercare was also similar. Having had a particularly difficult first birth, I felt I had some understanding of the anxiety and pain that went with recovery after GR surgery. I did reflect that although these trans women were born male, they will have an insight into the pain and dangers of childbirth through this experience that cis men cannot have. Childbirth and GR surgery are of course not the same thing, but there were definite parallels between the two.

The first few days were a blur to Ellen later when I asked her about them. She had her wooden cross with her in bed and a soft toy. She would wake up in the night asking for water or telling me that she had a dream. One time she woke up saying she felt a hand on her shoulder, and she was sure it was Jesus. I told her, 'If that's who you thought it was, it would have been Him. Don't doubt your feelings on this one.' Another time she said she had seen my mother. 'Mama Maryam came over and gave me a jam sandwich made with Iranian lavash bread, all rolled up.' This one brought tears to my eyes. Could it be that my mother knows all about Ellen now and is watching over her? Supporting me and Ellen at last with no prejudice or fear? I believe that Ellen had really seen my mother too.

We both tried hospital food. I sometimes tried the dishes Ellen didn't like. Sometimes I would eat her castoffs but generally, I'd go to the French bakery or restaurants in the concourse and bring back some food. We tried the humble pot noodle a couple of times too. The only rule was no vegetables or fruit as it was recommended that no one went to the toilet for the first week so as not to upset the surgeon's stitches.

After a couple of days, I was able to pop into the hotel which was a ten-minute drive away in the 'grab' taxis. I only managed to swim once in that first week. I had my showers in the hotel too. Then I learnt where the nearest large supermarket was. It was only fifteen minutes' walk from the hotel. There I found some nice little surprises. They had beautiful sarongs for less than five pounds which I bought for

Ellen for when she would leave the hospital. On my first visit, I bought a Pez dispenser and sweets. It was Sonic the Hedgehog. We had lots of childhood memories with Pez dispensers. Ellen laughed when she saw it.

The patients were able to chat together online using their iPads or laptops. Ellen called her friend Sally next door and showed her how to use a Pez dispenser like it was a YouTube training video. The whole thing was really funny when we watched it a few days later because the drugs had made Ellen's speech and movements slow. I bought another Pez dispenser for Sally. In the hotel we also watched the Seinfeld episode about a Pez dispenser. I think the whole Pez thing was a comfort for both of us and a welcome distraction. It was a reminder of a happy time in both our lives and a bit of fun as well.

I generally used to go out when I could and buy silly things for Ellen or her friends. The odd bag of Haribo or some cartoon stickers for Ellen's journal. Ellen was improving every day.

There are many occasions when we distract ourselves with trivial concerns just to avoid tackling our true challenges. That week in the hospital will always be a time I remember when I could give my full attention to the most important thing that was happening in my life. I see it as a blessing to have been in that position.

Torrents of Emotion

There was of course a deeply emotional side to our stay in the hospital. Ellen and I got to know each other better than we had ever done. As I looked at her asleep or even just sitting up writing in her journal, I reflected on how much I loved my children. There was a tightness in my chest when I saw her like that; vulnerable and to me, innocent. She had suffered quietly without even her own family fully understanding what she was going through.

دردی که انسان را به سکوت وا میدارد

بسیار سنگین تر از دردیست که

انسان را به فریاد وا میدارد....!

و انسانها فقط

به فریاد هم می رسند، نه به سکوت هم

A pain which forces people into silence

Is much harder to bear than the pain which,

Causes them to cry out with full force.

And people only

Attend to each other's cries, not each other's silence.

Forough Farrokhzad (1934 – 1967)

Before we went to Thailand together, I knew that Ellen did not talk to me about her private life or the emotions that go with being transgender. I thought it was up to her to initiate such conversations. I didn't want to pry. Maybe I was a little afraid too. If there was any fear, on my part, it was the fear of Ellen thinking of me as someone who doesn't understand or support her. I was afraid that I would say the wrong thing and drive her away.

As I began to talk with Ellen and the other trans women in Thailand however, I came across the issue of 'shame' which I had not even considered before. It made my heart ache when they spoke of the shame they felt when going about their normal lives in their respective countries.

They spoke of films in which trans women are portrayed as strange, cross-dressing males who get 'found out.' I remembered a scene in Crocodile Dundee. There must be many others too. They also spoke of being stared at as something that made them feel ashamed. I had imagined stares as causing fear but not shame.

Having said all this, the trans women I met embraced their identity whole heartedly. Afterall, they had all taken the brave step of going through the GR surgery. It was the reaction of society however, that made them feel uncomfortable and even threatened.

One of them, Hilary was a catwalk model. She was striking in her beauty and open about her gender. She had a boyfriend who was a cis male and pan-sexual.

At one time, these words had meant nothing to me other than annoying little expressions created by modern western culture. Now, I could see how defining people in this way gave a clarity to discussions about personal relationships.

I understood that increasingly more cis men are in relationships with trans women. Something that was far less common while I was growing up as a young adult in the UK. Ellen had told me that the French footballer Kylian Mbappé, has a trans partner. The numbers are not large, but it's good to see that younger generations are not bound by the same prejudices as previous ones. This means there is hope for the future. A future where we think of each other as human beings worthy of love irrespective of the shape of our bodies or what we used to look like.

Another trans woman I met was Zoe who firmly believed that the best way to live as a trans woman was to pass as a cis woman. I said I was not sure about that. 'Surely, the best outcome would be that society accepts trans women as exactly who they are. This has happened over many decades with the gay community – although we have a long way to go even with that one.' The whole idea to me had echoes of descendants of African American slaves 'passing as white.'

It is wrong for the transgender community to be made to feel like they had to blend in rather than celebrate their individuality but am I being too proscriptive here? Who am I to judge whether a trans person should try to pass as cis or not? Freedom of expression is after all a basic human right.

This expression has to be a free choice, however. No one should be made to alter their image because they feel ashamed of themselves for the way the look or because they fear persecution. It is a travesty that total strangers do not stop to think about the effect of their behaviour on others who have done them no harm.

*****

There was a 7-Eleven near the hotel that we all went to a few times a week for basic supplies. I never arranged to go there with anyone but usually bumped into people on my way there or back. The conversations we had on these walks have become special memories for me.

One time I was with Benita who was also British. She said she thought it was so good that I had accepted Ellen. She said her own parents did not want to know her even though some aunts and uncles and other relatives had no problems with her being trans. Benita has a son herself and an ex-wife who has now remarried. She spoke of her son with great affection. He was eight years old and happy with his two mums.

Benita talked of the shame she felt. I was shocked to hear this. She was such a lovely, softly spoken woman with a good job as a software engineer. She was the type of person that you get on well with from the start, but she talked of this shame. She said her parents had added to her shame by not accepting her. She spoke of when some Thai street vendors had told her she was beautiful and just when she said thank you, they had asked whether she was a man. I tried to reassure her, 'Well, you know, so close to the clinic, people see a lot of trans women go past. They would not have said this to upset you. Trans women are more like a wonder to them than anything else. Thai culture is different to ours.' I genuinely believed what I said.

I told Benita that I had lost a son. I said that that loss has focused my mind on how precious one's child is. My baby was taken away so suddenly, I did not have any chance to strike any bargains with God or to make any sacrifices to keep him alive. I knew there and then that I would have loved him no matter what life he chose for himself, what he chose to look like, or what gender or sexuality he had. I also knew that I would have done anything to make sure that he is happy and lives a fulfilling, authentic life. I had only wanted him to grow up and not die before me.

I can fully understand a parent's concern when they find out that one of their children is transgender. It is a huge issue. More so for the child than anyone else. The parent can either add to the problems of their child at this stage or walk with them in their time of need.

Many of us forget that we are only the centre of our children's lives for the first eighteen or twenty years of their lives. Their future partners and close friends usually get to spend more time with them than their parents. So, it would make sense to let our children choose the life they want. We will not be living that life. It is a life that belongs to them. It is their story, not ours. Like my eldest daughter said, 'This is about them, not us.'

*****

Looking at Ellen, in her bed, asleep in the hospital. I was so happy that I was there. I could not have survived my own troubled thoughts, had I not come with her. I could not bear to think of one of my children with no refuge, no mother with them under these conditions. I imagined myself in Ellen's shoes and felt the loneliness. Those emotions are ones that I shall never forget.

تکیه کن بر شانه ام؛ ای شاخه نیلوفری رنگ

تا غم بی تکیه گاهی را به چشمانت نبینم.

O! Lotus coloured branch! Lean on my shoulder.

So that I do not see in your eyes, the sorrow of not having a refuge.

From the song 'Tekyegah' sung by Sattar

*****

As all these chats, thoughts and feelings swam through my mind and body, I focused on my fears of telling Iranian relatives of Ellen's transition. I suddenly realised that I no longer had any fear or their judgement. Even if it meant that unkind words would be said about Ellen, I knew I would stand by her with full force and put any person who spoke with prejudice, in their place. The strength I felt was unshakeable. I had gained a new level of understanding from spending time in the company of trans women. This insight was only made possible because I had put prejudice aside.

All that said, I also knew that my father who is my closest relative of the older generation, was too ill to be told the news. That was a risk I still didn't think I could take.

At times like this, one cannot help but wish for a supportive parent. I longed for my father's support, but at the same time I also felt the pain of not being able to share my newfound strength with my parents. I was in need of a refuge myself.

Here, There and Everywhere

We tried to keep Ellen's hair tidy in hospital, but it was quite difficult! Ponytails would become undone. French plait was the same. The whole curly mass became like a lump on the back of her head. I tried combing it with my fingers from time to time. As I did that, I thought of how I did not want to be anywhere else in the world at that moment. I was just in exactly the right place at the right time.

'There, running my hands through her hair...'

The whole Beatles song unravelled in my head as I did this. This song was the only song in my head for the rest of my stay in Thailand. It became the song for Ellen and me, the song for this trip. Once we played it and hugged and cried.

She had changed my life 'with a wave of her hand'. I felt that I was a different person because of Ellen. In this land, among its kind, gentle people, I had learnt that the 'big deals' in life are only so because we make them into something they don't deserve to be. I could have tried to stop Ellen being herself, I could have threatened and got angry like some other parents. I could have had any number of hostile reactions to stop her being herself. But it was so much more natural, easy, and harmonious to accept her trust in her own feelings.

This song never left me all the time that I was in Thailand. I found myself singing it aloud sometimes. The chambermaid at the hotel found me quite amusing, I think; this singing mum from the UK who didn't look British. She used to call me 'sexy madam'. Once she even drew an hourglass silhouette with her hands when she said it. I laughed out loud. I told her she was sexy too. That became her name for me while I was there. Every morning, I would be greeted with, 'Good morning sexy madam.' I liked this daily exchange. It made me feel more alive somehow. It also made me smile to think that hotel staff in the UK would of course never call a guest sexy to their face, let alone use the word in exchange for their name.

The nurses and clinic staff on the other hand, called me, 'mummy.' I liked that for a different reason. They were so kind to Ellen that I felt like they were part of our family in Thailand. The family of all these trans girls and their companions. It was nice to be called 'mummy' by these beautiful Thai women that I may never see again but who had made such a lasting, positive difference to my daughter's life.

The ward sister made a particular impression on us. I will always remember her beautiful face lighting up when I asked her to show us how to wear a sarong I had bought for Ellen. She stepped into the middle of the roll of fabric, then she tied it around her waist finishing with a Thai curtsey and bringing her hands together with her head bowed. When she looked up, she was beaming with a gentle smile.

Ellen asked me to buy some fresh flowers for the nurses as a leaving present. We found a florist near the hospital. It was supposed to be a fifteen-minute walk, but I still managed to get lost even though I was using a navigation app. On the way there, I found a dressmakers' shop. There were at least ten people sewing garments in a small space. I made a mental note of the place.

Using various hand gestures, google translate and the shop website, I managed to let the florist know which bouquet I wanted. It was not cheap but then we had chosen quite English flowers: pink roses, blue hydrangea, large white carnations, and gypsophila. There were no flowers on display in the shop. The shop assistants had to fetch them from a fridge at the back. It was expensive business keeping flowers fresh in the heat of Thailand.

The bouquet was a great hit. When I brought it back, Ellen said, 'It's in trans colours as well!' Up to then, I had not known that pale pink, light blue and white are trans colours. We have a lovely picture of the beautiful ward sister holding the flowers.

The grace and kindness with which the medical staff carried out their duties had a normalising effect on my experience in the hospital. There was no judgement in their attitude. They were just nurses looking after their patients.

The Breakfasts

Once Ellen left the hospital, we became a firm part of the hotel community. The highlight of our days was the breakfast. It was a time when we met new arrivals and exchanged tips about the town and the whole experience. The girls also talked of post-op difficulties they were having, most of which were minor issues.

We shared breakfast foods that we had brought over as a comfort from our respective countries. The British had Marmite and English Breakfast tea, Australians had vegemite, the Danish had rye bread. These were small luxuries, but it was nice to have a taste of home in the morning.

There was an egg station where you could have any kind of egg cooked to order. I liked the way the eggs were fried. They were broken into shimmering hot oil so that when they were cooked, they had a golden crust around the edge. This is also how Iranians make fried eggs.

There was also the usual continental breakfast and an array of rice, noodles and stir fries for those who preferred Thai breakfasts.

*****

Family conflicts came up as a conversation topic now and then. One girl said her parents didn't even know she was in Thailand. Another said that she had not seen her parents for five years since she came out as trans.

There was an in-between reaction whereby the parents had not rejected their daughter, but had said things like, 'Your life will be very difficult. You couldn't find a job. You couldn't find a life partner.' This may have been true a few decades ago.

But times have changed now. We all know that our trans children are not choosing an easy path. My attitude is that it is best in all cases not to predict doom and gloom. If a person feels loved by their closest family, they can accomplish anything. They can break any number of taboos.

By way of contrast, there were four other mums who had accompanied their daughters. Three of them were teachers – that would be four teachers out of five mums including myself. The other mum was a beekeeper. I had a brief chat with her at a coffee table on the hotel patio. She was happy that she had come but was also anxious to get back to her other children and her bees and her farmers' market in Australia. We both talked about how we had immediately volunteered to come on the trip without asking what it involved. We had stepped into a situation we did not know anything about. The post-op recovery was a big surprise to us both. We hadn't realised the amount of physiotherapy that was needed.

One Australian girl had both her parents with her. Her dad was a typical Aussie man and a carpenter by profession. He happily joined in with the conversations about male and female organs. We all missed him when he left. He was the only male in our group. It was a shame that more dads hadn't come. It was such a support for the mum to have her husband with her. That couple also travelled around a bit together once their daughter was out of hospital. They were great fun to have around.

One of the girls said she did not want her mother there. She said her mum made a big fuss and worried too much. They felt if their mother was there, they would have had another person to worry about. I remembered my own mother when

I was in labour for my first child and how worried I was for her because she was fretting over me and looked like she was about to burst into crying.

*****

All topics were on the table at breakfast. Among the specifically trans topics, the issue of separate toilets for trans individuals came up once. The general consensus was that only half a percent of the population is trans. The media making a fuss about terrible things that can happen if trans women are allowed to use female toilets was upsetting to all.

The mention of certain extremely rare cases in headline news also promoted a negative image of trans individuals – one being the case of a prisoner who was convicted of rape but was now identifying as a woman and the issue of whether they should go to an all-male prison or not.

But discussions could be quite diverse. I managed to get my penny's worth in about the 'Woman-Life-Freedom' revolution in Iran and LGBTQ persecutions under the Islamic Republic.

There was an obvious interest in the peaceful attempts for the overthrow of the clergy in Iran and the way men had stepped up to support women. With Iranian opposition leaders already speaking of the establishment of a secular democracy and equality for all citizens including LGBTQ individuals, I said that there was great hope for the future of this community in Iran.

Some of the girls knew trans women who had gone to Iran for their GR surgery. I wondered what that experience would have been like. I have to say there were no horror stories told with respect to these surgeries.

I reflected later that if the person going to Iran for GR surgery is sure of being trans and they are not Iranian nationals, they may well have a good experience in Iran. Afterall, they will not have to stay in Iran and live there as a trans individual.

We also talked about early Islamic history once. I don't think there was much sympathy for organised religion among the group, but I do think most of the trans women there were spiritual people.

*****

The girls at the hotel were by no means masculine. Even those who were tall, just looked like tall women. Some had had facial surgery, but then, that is not uncommon among cis women these days either.

It was interesting to hear how each person manifested their transgender identity. There were some who just wanted to be left alone. They did not want to explain to anyone that they are transgender, but they did not hide the fact either. A minority preferred to 'pass' as cis women. Others were completely open and frank, sometimes even brazen in expressing their gender status.

One girl had gone to all the coffee shops and bars she frequented before coming to Thailand to let them know she was going to be away for a few months 'to get a vagina.'

Another had resigned from her job so as not to have to explain to her boss that she needed time off for GR surgery.

The boss in question had been very understanding, he had not only given her the time off 'for an operation,' but had offered her a large raise should she decide to come back to the same job. This was another software engineer who was clearly too good at what she did.

*****

Breakfast was a time for me to chat to other mums as well.

A couple of days after Ellen came out of hospital, I made a new friend in a Danish mum, Patricia, and her stunning daughter Maria. Patricia and I exchanged life stories during one breakfast all in a space of fifteen minutes. Maria was her only child, so they were rarely separated. We didn't go anywhere together but became friends over breakfast chats.

Once I found a tin of Danish butter biscuits in the supermarket which I bought for Patricia because it had Thai writing on. I thought it would be a good souvenir to take back. It was then that I saw how much she was missing Denmark. Her eyes filled with tears as she talked of the soldiers that were pictured on the tin with uniform very similar to the British Coldstream Guards. She said, 'They march every day in Copenhagen.' I said, 'How lovely! They reminded me of the tin soldier in The Nutcracker.' Maria said, 'Exactly!' Patricia is a teacher too. We have stayed in touch. That hotel was truly a haven for our girls and although we were both happy to be home afterwards, we miss that atmosphere of meeting kindred spirits every day.

Incidentals

During my four-week stay in Thailand, Ellen and I were for the most part in our hotel room so she could rest and recuperate. It was only towards the end of this period that Ellen became more mobile and was able to go on short walks outside the hotel.

However, this did not mean that I spent every minute of every day with Ellen. My days in the hotel were a mixture of supporting Ellen and going about the normal stuff of life at the same time. When I look back at those few weeks, I can see a lot of significance in the seemingly incidental activities and encounters that took place.

It was as if Ellen's healing was the background to these other happenings. If it hadn't been for these distractions, I don't know how we would have coped. It was good to be able to have a break from each other now and then. I think we would have both gone rather mad had we just stayed in our room together all the time.

The Sudoku book I bought in Britain came in very handy. It was well used by both me and Ellen. The hotel staff found this funny as I would go downstairs to a table in the lobby with my Sudoku book every day while Ellen was visited by the nurse or worked on her physiotherapy. I usually got a wink and a smile accompanied by the word 'Sudoku!' from hotel staff.

Sudoku became a life saver because it was a way for us to retreat into our left brain. These short breaks from the many emotions that occupied our minds, were not just welcome, they were necessary.

The nurses visited once every day in the morning. They just checked that everything was alright with the patients. They typically stayed for around fifteen minutes or longer if needed.

Shopping for lunches and snacks and doing the laundry were my only domestic duties. Even then, we gave all larger laundry items to the hotel laundry.

We used to have ham sandwiches for lunch regularly. The ham was German, and it was a kind of smoked, compressed, sliced meat. I used to buy Thai fruit too. This was a kind of a cultural lesson as this was so different to the fruit we were used to. Our favourite was pomelo segments straight from the fridge.

My other pastime was checking tweets about Iran. I only read the Persian language ones that came directly from Iran. Sometimes I would translate an important one into English but often I just liked and retweeted to keep certain hashtags going. I am still doing that daily. It has become a ritual. I shall only give up when the Woman-Life-Freedom revolution succeeds.

Sometimes trans individuals posted from Iran. I remember reading a disturbing account of a trans woman who was picked up by the so-called 'morality police.' She got into their van and immediately the men started hinting at a planned sexual assault. Then she got so scared that she vomited all over them! At that point they stopped the car and threw her out. It was a horrendous story, but I was glad that she got away.

My plans for swimming went out of the window. I only managed a few swims while I was in the hotel. It was hard to keep to a routine.

*****

Looking back, in terms of my own mental health, I had good days and not so good days. I was prone to occasional bouts of anxiety, sadness and a couple of times, anger. None of this was directed at anyone. It was all a sign of my frustration with things that had or hadn't happened that day.

On reflection, these feelings were side effects of me trying to appear calm and in control. I did not want to be that worried, fretting mother. There would be emotions bubbling inside that I would quash, but then they would find a way to burst out now and then. I tried to shield Ellen from this but there were a couple of times when she saw me at my worst.

*****

One activity that cheered me up was going to the local material shop and from there to the dressmakers that I had discovered on the way to the florist. A friend back in Britain who had lived in Thailand had told me to look out for good dressmakers. I had taken an old coat with me to be re-lined just in case I found a dressmaker. As it was, I managed to have copies made of two of my favourite summer dresses and got the old coat mended beautifully for very little money. The only problem with this whole venture was that while the dresses were with the dressmaker, I had to keep washing and wearing the same stuff for a few days!

*****

In my few interactions with Thai people I was time and again struck by their mindful respect for people and objects. I remember taking my glasses in to be mended. The optician promptly fixed them and presented them to me with both hands and a smile. I thanked him and asked for a case for the glasses. He gave me a blue case, and a yellow cloth for cleaning the glasses for free. He would not take any money no matter how much I insisted. Then his assistant wrapped the glasses in the cloth as if she was putting them to bed. She then folded the arms of the glasses over the cloth, put them in the case and gently closed the lid. She presented the case to me with both hands, a curtsey, and a smile. I now look after those glasses better than I ever did.

There is something in the Thai attitude to material possessions which is considered and respectful. It was an eye-opening experience for me to see how much care was put into mending and preserving old things. There were people on the high street who earnt their living by mending shoes and altering clothing. They were always busy when I went past.

The time spent in the care and repair of objects is a time well spent in thinking creatively and aiming for a positive, wholesome outcome. All this is not only a constructive activity, but it could serve to boost a person's mental health. The setting and achieving of small targets is a recognised way of combatting depression.

Western throw away culture is not just wasteful; it also engenders a lack of respect for the importance of objects in our lives. The objects we collect, and use can outlive us if we look after them well. They could become a link with who we were for our descendants.

The care and consideration afforded to objects also helps to slow the pace of life. The time spent carefully putting a pair of glasses in their case is a mindful time. If we expand that behaviour to all the things around us, we end up with far less time spent being fretful or anxious.

Some religions even believe in objects having souls. I personally think that there is a part of the people who have touched and used an object that lives on in our most treasured possessions.

*****

Our evenings were fun in the room. Ellen and I used to often watch Star Trek: The Next Generation or sometimes a movie. I can recommend a Turkish comedy called *Aile Arasında* – 'Among the Family', which features a trans woman as one of its main characters.

We mostly ordered food on the 'grab' app. This did not always work out well although we got the hang of it in time. Problems appeared mainly when we used websites that did not have any English translation for the food.

I never missed English or Persian food while I was in Thailand. Thai food is delicious, but I think it is also very much in harmony with the climate. While I was there, I could not imagine eating anything else. It seemed that the fresh spicy meat, vegetable and seafood dishes and the exotic fruit were all the sustenance that the body required.

Of all the Thai food that we tried, my favourites remain Tom Yum Soup, Papaya Salad and Thai Basil Pork with Jasmine rice and a fried egg on top complete with green beans and the crunchy, golden crust around the egg.

The Beach House

Dr. Suporn has a beach house. All post-op patients are invited to this house for a lunch and a Thai massage every other Wednesday. On the way to the beach house, we also stopped at a coffee shop owned by the daughter of Dr Suporn.

Everyone looked forward to this trip. It is fair to say that all patients were suffering with a bit of cabin fever. They had not been totally immobile after the operation, but their movement was limited. For Ellen even the walk from the hotel room to the lift was slow. In the early days, I had to support her while she did this walk.

We all knew that the Beach House trip was part of their recovery. It was there to give them the confidence that they could be as active as they had been before the operation. For all of us the departure from the hustle and bustle of Chon Buri was also a welcome break.

We went there in a couple of air-conditioned, black minivans. The coffee shop was by the beach too. It was set in a beautiful Thai villa with a lovely garden and the sea just across the road. Ellen and I had Thai iced tea and sat in the garden which was full of all colours of hibiscus that I did not know existed until then. We chatted and took pictures and breathed in the fresh sea air.

Between the coffee shop and the beach house, we saw a lot of urban monkeys just walking about or eating out of rubbish bins. Some had babies. The driver kept shouting, 'Monkey!' Which made us laugh. Everyone was relaxed and happy. We all felt a bit more normal.

There was a short driveway leading to the beach house which had tiles the shape of large butterflies worked into the ground. Everyone liked this as the butterfly is one of the symbols of the clinic; all to do with trans women emerging from a cocoon into their true selves.

The house was decorated in a traditional style. All the wood including the flooring and the staircase was teak. There were plenty of sofas and easy chairs in the sitting room to help recovering patients. The soft furnishings were made of beautiful Thai material as were the mats that we lay on for the massages. It was a beautiful place.

On the veranda outside the house, there was also a nice buffet laid out for our lunch. Salads and jasmine rice and Thai barbequed chicken.

A set of steps led down to the beach through a lush, cool garden. The plants that made the most impression on me were the Frangipani trees which I had never seen before. The flowers were either pink or white with a yellow centre. I thought the smell was heavenly although one Australian trans woman said that they had these plants in Australia, and she hated the smell.

Ellen was not yet well enough to navigate the garden or the steps so while she rested inside the cool, airconditioned house, I went down the steps to the beach on my own.

Rebecca was there already. She was a gentle person with an unusual history. She had been in the US Army for seven or eight years and had served in Afghanistan and Iraq on a few tours. She also had a wife and three children of whom she was very fond. She had made it down to the beach even though her surgery was a day after Ellen's. I was collecting shells because that's what I usually do on beaches. Rebecca joined me. It turned out that she was into making jewellery as well as her many other talents. She gave me some good tips on how to make earrings and necklaces out of the shells. I still haven't got round to that, but the shells are sitting on the dining table in my house even as I type this.

We walked back to the house. One of our drivers had brought fresh, green coconuts and a large machete to the patio. He prepared us one each and of course the juice was delicious and cooling in the thirty-degree heat. Three people were already in for massages. I went in with the last group of three. The massage was gentler than I expected but I felt the positive effects of it for the next few days as bits of my neck and back creaked into place. I had been supporting a tense neck and back ache until that day.

At the beach house I had a chance to talk with a Japanese trans woman whom I had met but had not spoken with. She was there with a male support person. I never found out if he was her brother or her partner. We were able to communicate through an incredible gadget that she had. This handheld machine could translate the spoken word from any language into another one. So, I spoke into it in Persian which was then translated into Japanese. I asked them if they knew of Sahel Rosa, an Iranian Japanese actress who has an incredible story of coming from a horror-stricken childhood to be a spokesperson for refugees and the Iranian diaspora. They said they didn't know her but will look her up.

On the way back, everyone was even more relaxed because of the massages, being out in the fresh sea air and eating good food. We talked about how nice it was to do something resembling a holiday activity. The trip to Chon Buri had not been a holiday for any of us. Our outings had all consisted of running errands across town and taxi rides to the clinic and the hospital while the time in the hotel was being spent on lots of post-operation physiotherapy and chats about recovery. Eva from Germany said that they should all get T-shirts saying, 'I went to Thailand and all I got was a vagina.' I found that comment hilarious, partly because it was so true.

Guides, Teachers, and Holy Men

During my last week in Chon Buri, I half-decided to go to Bangkok just for a day visit. On the day however, I kept changing my mind. I partly felt guilty about being a tourist for the day while Ellen was stuck in the hotel, but I also worried about leaving her on her own.

In the end, Ellen insisted and everyone else in the hotel said they would look out for her. So, I decided to get myself a 'grab' taxi and go. The only problem was that I had lost half a day. The only tour I could book, did not take bookings for single people, so I had to pay double but as things turned out, the experience was worth the money.

I was the only person on the tour, so I got VIP treatment and had many pleasant conversations with the guide, Sam who spoke very good English and was extremely knowledgeable about Thai history of which I was completely ignorant. Sam also told me that he had never met anyone from Iran before. I realised that I had to be on best behaviour. This was going to be his first impression of Iran after all.

The Three Temples' Tour covered 'Wat Traimit': Temple of the Golden Buddha, 'Wat Phra Chetuphon': Temple of the Reclining Buddha and 'Wat Arun': Temple of Dawn.

The car was air conditioned and comfortable. At our first stop, I saw The Golden Buddha, which weighed 5.5 tonnes and was made of pure gold. I was astounded by all the gold I saw that day.

Sam explained that the Golden Buddha was saved by a man who had covered it with plaster to dupe the Burmese invaders who were taking any gold they found to Burma. The man in question lost his life protecting this Buddha. It seemed that the Burmese had caused a lot of devastation in Thailand some three hundred years ago. I asked if there was still any animosity between the Thai and the Burmese people. I explained that in Iran, people still harbour ill feeling towards invaders of the past. Sam just said, 'No, we don't bear grudges because we believe in Karma.' A nice philosophy to have; it saves people from a lot of needless rumination, hatred and even wars.

There were garlands of jasmine and marigold displayed at the entrance to the temple and saffron robes of the kinds that Buddhist monks wear. In return of a suggested donation of one hundred Bhat – about two pounds and fifty pence – these items could be presented at the Buddha's feet for the use of the monks in the temple. Sam was surprised when I said I would take some jasmine and a robe. My mother loved jasmine and jasmine was also Ellen's princess, so it was important for me to give that offering of thanks.

Next, we went to see The Reclining Buddha. This statue was mind boggling. It reminded me of an old film called 'The Thief of Baghdad,' which I loved as child. There is a giant statue in a huge cave in that film. The Reclining Buddha took up an entire huge room as big as a cathedral. It was laying down along the length of the building.

The walls in all the temples I saw were also beautifully and ornately decorated. The buildings were out of this world and a wonder to behold.

In the last temple we saw statues depicting the different stages of Buddha's life. I started chatting to Sam about ancient Iran and how the Buddha was almost a contemporary of Cyrus the Great.

'You see, as well as being a king, Cyrus was a kind of a holy man. He was venerated in the Old Testament for freeing Jewish people from captivity in Babylon and rebuilding the Temple in Jerusalem. The book of Isiah calls him 'The Anointed One.'

So, there are parallels with the Buddha and Cyrus, both from royal blood and both holy men.'

Sam was listening with interest. He said all this was very interesting and he was going to read up on the history. He had not realised that Iran was the same place as Persia. He had always wondered where Persia was exactly. I said, 'Just like Thailand used to be called Siam, Iran used to be called Persia.' He smiled and he said, 'You are a teacher, aren't you?' I smiled back because I realised, I had slipped into teaching mode without noticing it myself.

Sam was a perceptive, intelligent, and kind man. He showed me how to meditate in the temple the way he had been taught by his own master as a child. He was interested in my reason for visiting Thailand and proud when I said that the surgeons in Chon Buri were some of the best in the world.

Just before we parted ways outside the last temple. There was a raised platform which I pointed to. I said, 'We have those in England, but they are lower. Are they for mounting horses?' Sam said, 'No! That is for mounting elephants. Horses do not have the same prestige here.' That comment made me smile. I was in a country where only elephants were good enough for royalty.

We both agreed that we had learnt a lot from each other. Sam said, 'We are in the same job really. I like to teach tourists the best things about Thailand, and you do the same for your students and Iran.' I felt like I was saying goodbye to a friend when he left.

Final Farewell

After I got back from Bangkok, the days rolled on quickly. Ellen was staying on for another two weeks, but her friend was coming to take over from me for a week and then my elder daughter was coming to take over from Ellen's friend. The two sisters were travelling back to Britain together.

My time in Thailand had coincided with my birthday, Mothers' Day, and Persian New Year. I had also missed my son's birthday. March is a busy month in our family.

The girls in the hotel sang happy birthday for me at breakfast. We also had a nice meal and cake in the evening., Ellen and I had pedicures on Mothers' Day. That was my last day in Chon Buri as well. I said goodbye to the friendly chambermaid and asked her to change the sheets because someone else was coming to take my place. When Ellen's friend arrived, we all went to dinner. Afterwards, I got in a taxi and went to Pattaya for a couple of days before leaving for Britain. By complete coincidence, the driver was a Thai trans woman.

Leaving Ellen was the hardest part. She was much better now, and I knew she would be alright, but I had become so used to being able to check on her every minute, that I had a bit of anxiety at the pit of my stomach. I knew it was an illogical feeling, but it was there.

Parvin E'tesami has these few lines in her poem, 'Kindness of God,' which is about the moment the mother of Moses floats the basket in the Nile. This is God speaking to her.

به که برگردی، به ما بسپاریش

کی تو از ما دوست تر می داریش؟

It is best that you return and entrust him to us.

Surely, you do not love him more than we do.

So, as I left Chon Buri, I entrusted my child to God.

There were big hugs from everyone as I left the hotel. Saying goodbye to Patricia was hard. We vowed to keep in touch. I had a lump in my throat, not just because I would miss Ellen, but because of everyone else as well. We had been a close community, almost a family, for a month. I had grown to love these brave girls and their gentle strength.

*****

In Pattaya, I met up with Amir, a friend of the family whom I had only seen once in Iran at my mother's funeral. He has lived in Pattaya for over a decade. It was good to be told about Thai customs and food in Persian by an Iranian. We even celebrated the Persian New Year together. We had the traditional Iranian herbed rice but with Thai salads and fried fish kindly provided by Amir.

Pattaya provided me with some rest that I had not had time for. I slept and I walked by the beach. I got lost in town once, making the Tuk Tuk drivers rich with all the unnecessary rides I went on. I smiled too much at a Thai trans woman who was out and about with her older European male partner. At first, she smiled back but then as I got lost in my thoughts of Chon Buri and couldn't stop smiling in her direction, I think she was annoyed at me. Then I had to jump out of the Tuk Tuk as I realised, I was yet again on the wrong route.

I chatted to Amir about this interaction. He said, 'What do you think about European men coming here and taking young Thai partners?' I had to think about this. 'It's their own business really. As long as they are happy, which they seem to be, and they are not harming anyone, why not?' Amir agreed. I told him when I saw the couple in the Tuk Tuk, I had no doubt that the man cared deeply for his partner. I could tell by the way he looked at her. It was a lovely thing to see.

One comment Amir made before I left, was that he thought that I was not in the business of judging people. I hope this is true about me. It is something I strive for. More than anything, my trip to Chon Buri taught me this was the best way to be.

It is best to spend one's time on earth loving people and not judging them.

To add a bit of Thai wisdom, if you have any urge to correct other people's behaviour, just remember that if what they are doing is harmful, Karma will take care of everything.

* * * * *

On the return flight, I reflected on how I set out with so many trepidations but was now feeling that I was so privileged to have had this experience. I thanked God for giving me this opportunity to see another aspect of what it is to be human and to have the reaffirmation that love is the answer to all challenges we face.

At Heathrow, I saw my partner's beaming smile as we spotted each other. I was beaming too. I had missed him and my other two children. It was good to be back with the rest of my family.

Much of my happiness, however, was because I knew that Ellen now had the best start to the rest of her life.

Other books by this author also available on Amazon

Aberu – kindle ebook

Maman – kindle ebook

Affinity – kindle ebook

Essay on Dual Identity – paperback (This book consists of the three above essays combined)

Transcultural is also available as a kindle ebook.

Printed in Great Britain
by Amazon

25793862R00052